Career
Counseling

Theories of Psychotherapy Series

Theories of Psychotherapy Series

Jon Carlson and Matt Englar-Carlson, Series Editors

Career
Counseling

Mark L. Savickas

American Psychological Association

Washington, DC

First Printing May 2011
Second Printing October 2013
Third Printing February 2018

Published by
American Psychological Association
750 First Street, NE
Washington, DC 20002
www.apa.org

To order
APA Order Department
P.O. Box 92984
Washington, DC 20090-2984
Tel: (800) 374-2721; Direct: (202) 336-5510 Fax: (202) 336-5502; TDD/TTY: (202) 336-6123
Online: www.apa.org/pubs/books/
E-mail: order@apa.org

In the U.K., Europe, Africa, and the Middle East, copies may be ordered from
American Psychological Association
3 Henrietta Street
Covent Garden, London
WC2E 8LU England

Typeset in Minion by Circle Graphics, Columbia, MD

Printer: United Book Press, Baltimore, MD
Cover Designer: Minker Design, Sarasota, FL
Cover Art: *Lily Rising*, 2005, oil and mixed media on panel in craquelure frame, by Betsy Bauer

The opinions and statements published are the responsibility of the authors, and such opinions and statements do not necessarily represent the policies of the American Psychological Association.

Library of Congress Cataloging-in-Publication Data

Savickas, Mark, 1947-
  Career counseling / Mark L. Savickas. — 1st ed.
    p. cm. — (Theories of psychotherapy series)
  Includes bibliographical references and index.
  ISBN-13: 978-1-4338-0980-4
  ISBN-10: 1-4338-0980-X
  1. Vocational guidance—Psychological aspects. 2. Career development—Psychological aspects. 3. Personality and occupation. I. Title.

HF5381.S279 2011
650.14—dc22
                            2011006285

British Library Cataloguing-in-Publication Data
A CIP record is available from the British Library.

Printed in the United States of America
First Edition

Dedicated to Mary Ann,
the heart of my life story

Contents

Series Preface

Some might argue that in the contemporary clinical practice of psychotherapy, evidence-based intervention and effective outcome have overshadowed theory in importance. Maybe. But, as the editors of this series, we don't propose to take up that controversy here. We do know that psychotherapists adopt and practice according to one theory or another because their experience, and decades of good evidence, suggests that having a sound theory of psychotherapy leads to greater therapeutic success. Still, the role of theory in the helping process can be hard to explain. This narrative about solving problems helps convey theory's importance:

> Aesop tells the fable of the sun and wind having a contest to decide who was the most powerful. From above the earth, they spotted a man walking down the street, and the wind said that he bet he could get his coat off. The sun agreed to the contest. The wind blew, and the man held on tightly to his coat. The more the wind blew, the tighter he held. The sun said it was his turn. He put all of his energy into creating warm sunshine, and soon the man took off his coat.

What does a competition between the sun and the wind to remove a man's coat have to do with theories of psychotherapy? We think this deceptively simple story highlights the importance of theory as the precursor to any effective intervention—and hence to a favorable outcome. Without a guiding theory we might treat the symptom without understanding the role of the individual. Or we might create power conflicts with our clients and not understand that, at times, indirect means of helping (sunshine) are often as effective—if not more so—than direct ones (wind). In the absence of theory, we might lose track of the treatment rationale and instead get caught up in, for example, social correctness and not wanting to do something that looks too simple.

What exactly *is* theory? The *APA Dictionary of Psychology* defines theory as "a principle or body of interrelated principles that purports to explain or predict a number of interrelated phenomena." In psychotherapy, a theory is a set of principles used to explain human thought and behavior, including what causes people to change. In practice, a theory creates the goals of therapy and specifies how to pursue them. Haley (1997) noted that a theory of psychotherapy ought to be simple enough for the average therapist to understand, but comprehensive enough to account for a wide range of eventualities. Furthermore, a theory guides action toward successful outcomes while generating hope in both the therapist and client that recovery is possible.

Theory is the compass that allows psychotherapists to navigate the vast territory of clinical practice. In the same ways that navigational tools have been modified to adapt to advances in thinking and ever-expanding territories to explore, theories of psychotherapy have changed over time. The different schools of theories are commonly referred to as waves, the first wave being psychodynamic theories (i.e., Adlerian, psychoanalytic), the second wave learning theories (i.e., behavioral, cognitive–behavioral), the third wave humanistic theories (person-centered, gestalt, existential), the fourth wave feminist and multicultural theories, and the fifth wave postmodern and constructivist theories. In many ways, these waves represent how psychotherapy has adapted and responded to changes in psychology, society, and epistemology as well as to changes in the nature of psychotherapy itself. Psychotherapy and the theories that guide it are dynamic and responsive. The wide variety of theories is also testament to the different ways in which the same human behavior can be conceptualized (Frew & Spiegler, 2008).

It is with these two concepts in mind—the central importance of theory and the natural evolution of theoretical thinking—that we developed the APA Theories of Psychotherapy Series. Both of us are thoroughly fascinated by theory and the range of complex ideas that drive each model. As university faculty members who teach courses on the theories of psychotherapy, we wanted to create learning materials that not only highlight the essence of the major theories for professionals and professionals in training but also clearly bring the reader up to date on the current status of the models. Often in books on theory, the biography of the original theorist overshadows the evolution of the model. In contrast, our intent is to highlight the contemporary uses of the theories as well as their history and context.

As this project began, we faced two immediate decisions: which theories to address and who best to present them. We looked at graduate-level theories of psychotherapy courses to see which theories are being taught, and we explored popular scholarly books, articles, and conferences to determine which theories draw the most interest. We then developed a dream list of authors from among the best minds in contemporary theoretical practice. Each author is one of the leading proponents of that approach as well as a knowledgeable practitioner. We asked each author to review the core constructs of the theory, bring the theory into the modern sphere of clinical practice by looking at it through a context of evidence-based practice, and clearly illustrate how the theory looks in action.

There are 24 titles planned for the series. Each title can stand alone or can be put together with a few other titles to create materials for a course in psychotherapy theories. This option allows instructors to create a course featuring the approaches they believe are the most salient today. To support this end, APA Books has also developed a DVD for each of the approaches that demonstrates the theory in practice with a real client. Many of the DVDs show therapy over six sessions. Contact APA Books for a complete list of available DVD programs (http://www.apa.org/pubs/videos).

It is hard to overestimate the effect of work on one's life. One of the core tasks of life is the development of vocational identity. Recent estimates indicate that American adults spend one third to one half of their waking hours at work. Further, the recent global economic downturn has driven home the value of work, negatively reflected in the stress, fear, and uncertainty associated with unemployment and significant changes in the nature of the structure of work. Since its inception, career counseling has traditionally worked from an objective perspective of matching a person's traits and interests with different aspects of a vocation in the hope of discovering a good match. In *Career Counseling*, Mark L. Savickas presents a new way of envisioning the practice of career counseling that is embedded in constructivist and narrative epistemology. It is not hyperbole to suggest that Dr. Savickas offers a paradigm shift in this field. The contemporary approach presented here is adaptive enough to match the rapidly changing and growing global economy, yet sensitive enough to place meaning-making and the influence of cultural forces as its centerpiece. The reader can expect a model that relates to the current vocational landscape yet offers notably useable counseling tools. From the beginning, we wanted Dr. Savickas's ideas and approach to be a part of the APA Theories of Psychotherapy Series. It has been an honor and pleasure to edit this book, and we are sure that readers will be excited and inspired by the model presented.

—Jon Carlson and Matt Englar-Carlson

REFERENCES

Frew, J., & Spiegler, M. (2008). *Contemporary psychotherapies for a diverse world.* Boston, MA: Lahaska Press.
Haley, J. (1997). *Leaving home: The therapy of disturbed young people.* New York, NY: Routledge.

How to Use This Book
With APA Psychotherapy Videos

Each book in the Theories of Psychotherapy Series is specifically paired with a DVD that demonstrates the theory applied in actual therapy with a real client. Many DVDs feature the author of the book as the guest therapist, allowing students to see eminent scholars and practitioners putting the theory they write about into action.

The DVDs have a number of features that make them useful for learning more about theoretical concepts:

- Many DVDs contain six full sessions of psychotherapy over time, giving viewers a chance to see how clients respond to the application of the theory over the course of several sessions.
- Each DVD has a brief introductory discussion recapping the basic features of the theory behind the approach demonstrated. This allows viewers to review the key aspects of the approach about which they have just read.
- DVDs feature actual clients in unedited psychotherapy sessions. This provides an opportunity to get a sense of the look and feel of real psychotherapy, something that written case examples and transcripts sometimes cannot convey.
- There is a therapist commentary track that viewers may choose to play during the psychotherapy sessions. This track gives insight into why therapists do what they do in a session. Further, it provides an in vivo opportunity to see how the therapist uses the model to conceptualize the client.

The books and DVDs may be used together as a teaching tool for showing how theoretical principles affect practice. The DVD *Career Counseling Over Time,* which features the author as the guest expert, provides an example of how this narrative approach looks in practice. In the six sessions on this DVD, Dr. Savickas works with two clients, both men in their 20s. One client just finished his college degree but finds that he has interests that fall outside his chosen field. The second client is a former Marine now working as a carpenter who wants to find a career in which he can more fully use his skills. By asking a series of questions to get the clients to tell their own stories, Dr. Savickas extracts pertinent themes, highlighting what the clients find most meaningful in life, and then works with them to apply these themes in creating their career paths.

Career
Counseling

1

The World of Work and Career Interventions

Work in the 21st century leaves people feeling anxious and insecure. Previously, the stable employment and secure organizations of the 20th century offered a firm basis for building a life and envisioning a future. Such stability and security have now given way to a new social arrangement of flexible work and fluid organizations, causing people tremendous distress (Kalleberg, 2009). This new arrangement sets workers adrift as they endeavor to chart their futures, shape their identities, and maintain relationships. Meanwhile, the global economy poses new questions about work lives—most especially, how may individuals negotiate a lifetime of job changes without losing their social identity and sense of self?

The "dejobbing" or "jobless work" that has accompanied the digital revolution changes long-term jobs into short-term projects, making it increasingly difficult to comprehend careers with theories that emphasize stability rather than mobility. The new employment market in an unsettled economy calls for viewing career not as a lifetime commitment to one employer but as selling services and skills to a series of employers who need projects completed. While the form of career changes from commitment to flexibility, so too must the form of career counseling change. Career theories and techniques must evolve to better assist workers throughout the world in adapting to fluid societies and flexible organizations. To better help clients design their lives in the 21st century, many career practitioners have begun to transform their practices (Savickas et al., 2009). They are supplementing the vocational guidance of modernity and the career education of high modernity with the career counseling of postmodernity.

Vocational guidance and career education rose to prominence because they effectively addressed the questions asked about work lives in earlier times (Guichard, 2005). The first important theory of vocational behavior emerged early in the 20th century to address a question asked by Western societies as they coped with industrialization, urbanization, and immigration: How may workers be efficiently matched to fitting work? The answer to this question came in Parsons's (1909) formula of matching a person's abilities and interests to an occupation's requirements and rewards. Over the next 5 decades, Parsons's model for matching individuals to jobs evolved into person–environment theory. Holland's (1997) congruence theory of vocational choice brought the matching model to its current pinnacle. Practitioners apply Holland's matching model when they perform vocational guidance to help clients (a) enhance self-knowledge, (b) increase occupational information, and (c) match self to occupation.

Following World War II, the United States experienced the rise of suburban, middle-class individuals employed by hierarchical bureaucracies located in horizontal skyscrapers. Consequently, in the middle of the 20th century a theory of vocational development emerged to address the question of how to climb the career ladders in hierarchical professions and bureaucratic organizations. Practitioners apply Super's (1957) model of vocational development when they perform career education to help clients (a) understand career stages; (b) learn about imminent developmental tasks; and (c) rehearse the attitudes, beliefs, and competencies needed to master those tasks. Holland's (1997) theory of vocational choice as applied in vocational guidance and Super's (1990) theory of vocational development as applied in career education remain useful today when considering how to match workers to occupations and how to develop careers within bureaucratic organizations.

However, as corporations changed shape at the dawn of the 21st century, the nexus of career moved from the organization to the individual (Hall, 1996a). Rather than *develop* a career within a stable organization, the digital revolution requires that individuals *manage* their own careers. This shift in responsibility from the organization to the individual posed the new question of how individuals may negotiate a lifetime of job changes. The theory of career construction (Savickas, 2001, 2005) emerged as one answer to this question. Practitioners apply career construction theory when they perform career counseling to (a) construct career through small stories, (b) deconstruct and reconstruct the small stories into a large story, and (c) coconstruct the next episode in the story.

EVOLUTION OF CAREER COUNSELING

Although the term *career counseling* has been bandied around since the 1960s, scholarly conceptualizations of the process have only recently drawn sustained attention (Subich & Simonson, 2001). A pivotal event in the evolution of career counseling theory occurred at the inaugural conference of the Society for Vocational Psychology (Savickas & Lent, 1994). During the conference, the participants concluded that theories of career development differed from theories of career counseling. Although many researchers and practitioners have regarded Holland's (1997) theory of types and Super's (1957) theory of stages as career counseling theories, types and stages are primarily theories of vocational choice and its development. In conducting actual career interventions, the profession of career counseling has relied on Parsons's (1909) matching model for vocational guidance as its core "counseling" model. The matching model calls for a client to make rational decisions after the counselor provides test interpretations and occupational information. This highly effective content approach to vocational guidance eventually was supplemented by a process approach to career education. The process model concentrates on how to make decisions, not on which occupation to choose. In applying the process model, practitioners teach clients the attitudes, beliefs, and competencies that lead to realistic decisions. Similar to *vocational guidance,* this process model of teaching developmental attitudes and competencies has also been called *career counseling,* although it is really *career education.* Career counseling requires a relationship dimension in addition to the communication dimension composing guidance and education (Crites, 1981).

To consider the lacunae in career counseling theories, the Society for Vocational Psychology hosted a second conference (Savickas & Walsh, 1996). The participants agreed that career development theories address the knowledge question of what we can know about a problem, whereas career counseling theories must address the action question of what clients may do about the problem. Osipow (1996) asserted that career development theories were not designed to provide operational procedures for use in career intervention. He wondered if practitioners expected too much from career development theories. Myers (1996) wondered if the schism between theory and practice might be due to misconceptualizing career development theories as counseling theories. The long-standing schism between personal counseling and career counseling (Subich, 1993) quickly became contextualized as misrepresenting vocational guidance as career counseling.

During the conference, two new career counseling theories were presented. Chartrand (1996) proposed developing career counseling models that incorporate and complement theories of career development. She offered a rudimentary career counseling theory that used sociocognitive career theory to address counseling content and an interactional component to address counseling process. In a similar vein, Krumboltz (1996) offered a counseling complement to his social learning theory of career decision making. Subsequently, Krumboltz (2009) elaborated that model into the happenstance learning theory of career counseling that concentrates on helping clients incorporate chance events into their career development. Pryor and Bright (2011) also concentrated on unplanned and chance events in formulating a chaos theory of careers with a complementary counseling model.

Rather than complementing an existing career development theory, Savickas (1996) converged career development theories by imposing a framework to highlight their linkages and then elaborated the implications for assessment and intervention. The convergence framework eventually evolved into a constructionist theory of vocational behavior focused on personality traits, developmental tasks, and life themes (Savickas, 2001). As the theory of career construction evolved, Savickas (2005) added an explicit model of career counseling. It is neither a model of vocational guidance that orients individuals to the world of work and their places in it nor a career education model that teaches clients about developmental tasks and rational coping. It is truly a counseling model because it concentrates on the interpersonal process of helping individuals construct careers. It meets Super's (1951) desiderata of career counseling as

> the process of helping a person to develop and accept an integrated and adequate picture of himself and of his role in world of work, to test this concept against reality, and to convert it into reality, with satisfaction to himself and benefit to society. (p. 92)

Counseling for career construction, or simply career counseling, does not replace but rather takes its place among the interventions of vocational guidance and career education. To succinctly explain counseling's place, Figure 1.1 outlines fundamental differences among guidance, education, and

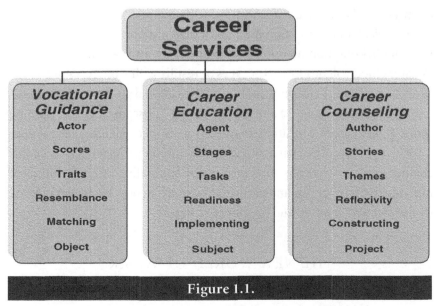

Figure 1.1.

Career services: A comparison of guidance, education, and counseling.

counseling as distinct career interventions. Vocational guidance, from the objective perspective of individual differences, views clients as actors who may be characterized by scores on traits and who may be helped to match themselves to occupations that employ people whom they resemble. Career education, from the subjective perspective of individual development, views clients as agents who may be characterized by their degree of readiness to engage developmental tasks appropriate to their life stages and who may be helped to implement new attitudes, beliefs, and competencies that further their careers. Career counseling, from the project perspective of individual design, views clients as authors who may be characterized by autobiographical stories and who may be helped to reflect on life themes with which to construct their careers. The three distinctions in Figure 1.1 are explained more fully in book chapters: McAdams and Olson (2010) differentiated actor, agent, and author; Savickas (2001) differentiated traits, themes, and tasks; and Savickas (2011) differentiated object, subject, and project.

So today, depending upon a client's needs, practitioners may apply different career services: vocational guidance to identify occupational fit, career education to foster vocational development, or career counseling to design a work life. Each career intervention—whether it be guidance, education, or counseling—is valuable and effective for its intended purpose. As practitioners select an intervention for a particular situation, they answer anew the essential question first posed by Williamson and Bordin (1941, p. 8): What method will produce what types of results with what types of clients? Readers interested in learning more about vocational guidance may consult Holland (1997) or Lofquist and Dawis (1991). Those interested in learning more about career education may consult Super, Savickas, and Super (1996). The current book is about career counseling. The remainder of this chapter explains why constructionist career counseling meets the needs of individuals preparing for and participating in the new world of work forged by the digital revolution and the global economy.

THE NEW WORLD OF WORK

During the 1st decade of the 21st century, Western societies experienced a break with previous forms of work and occupations. Rapid advances in information technology and opening of world markets produced a glob-alization that is reshaping forms of work and transforming ways of living. Although full-time employment remains a dominant form of work and long-term careers still exist, temporary and part-time work are increas-ingly commonplace following the flattening of hierarchical organizations. The digital revolution requires that organizations become smaller, smarter, and swifter in responding to market conditions. This has been accom-plished by reducing layers of decision making and removing barriers between functional units to produce what Welch (1992), then president of General Electric, called a "boundaryless" organization.

Changing the shape of organizations changes the shape of careers. The employee in a postmodern 21st-century organization becomes unbounded and ungrounded. Now organizations mix standard jobs with nonstandard assignments. Work has not disappeared, but dejobbing has affected its structure by shaping work as an assignment that begins as a project and ends with a product. A prime example of work as a project is making a motion picture. For that project, the producers assemble a large team of specialists with diverse skills to work for a set period of time to make a movie. When the movie wraps, the team disassembles, with each member seeking employ-ment on another project. For many workers, an assignment does not last even 2 years. More than half of the individuals born after 1980 left their first job within 5 months (Saratoga Institute, 2000). This was true not only for emerging adults but also for those adults who in previous times had stabi-lized in jobs and families. Of the jobs started by workers between the ages of 33 and 38, 39% ended in less than a year and 70% ended in fewer than 5 years. One in four workers has been with his or her current employer for less than a year (Bureau of Labor Statistics, 2004).

INSECURE WORKERS

As projects replace jobs, working in the postmodern global economy involves frequent dislocations from employment assignments that give meaning and significance to life (Kalleberg, 2009). Of course, uncertainty and anxiety accompany the recurrent transitions between assignments.

Thus, the dejobbing of organizations has produced the "insecure worker," including employees who are called *temporary, contingent, casual, contract, freelance, part-time, external, atypical, adjunct, consultant,* and *self-employed.* Working in these roles does not provide the benefits of a traditional job. Once taken for granted, matters such as job security, health insurance, and pensions have become problematic. Even the American Dream of owning a home is fading for many workers. Today's mobile workforce is better off renting a place to live because home ownership ties people to one geographic location with its limited range of employers. I do note that careers bounded by bureaucratic organizations still exist for many people. Nevertheless, we have entered the age of insecure workers who are no longer bounded by a single organization and grounded in the same job for 3 decades.

Existing career theories do not adequately account for the uncertain and rapidly changing occupational structure, nor do they address the needs of peripheral and external workers. Even for core workers, there is a decline in identifiable and predictable career routes. Established paths and traditional scripts are dissolving. Rather than developing a stable life based on secure employment, most workers today must maintain flexible employability through lifelong learning or, as some say, "learn for a living." Rather than developing a career by making plans in a stable medium, they must manage a career by noticing possibilities in a changing environment.

CAREER THEORIES AND INTERVENTIONS FOR THE 21ST CENTURY

Twentieth-century institutions provided a metanarrative for the life course, a story with coherence and continuity. The metanarrative clearly outlined trajectories with stable commitments around which individuals planned their lives. The 21st-century organizational narrative about career is uncertain and insecure, so individuals cannot make life plans around institutional commitments (Kalleberg, 2009). Their compass for action must point to possibilities in a fluid world rather than predictions in a stable society. Because boundaryless organizations provide individuals with so little career structure, individuals now must take more responsibility for managing their own work lives. Rather than living a narrative conferred by a corporation, people must author their own stories as they navigate occupational transitions in the postmodern world.

In an article titled "Holding Environments at Work," Kahn (2001) asserted that career theories need to address the emergence of boundaryless organizations. *Protean* and *boundaryless* are two metaphors that symbolize the new career, one now owned by the person rather than the organization. Realizing that the individual rather than the organization shapes a 21st-century career, Hall (1996b) formulated the concept of a protean career. As an adjective, *protean* means flexible, versatile, and adaptive. Hall described a protean career as self-directed and shaped by intrinsic rather than extrinsic values. In the pursuit of self-directed values, the individual uses the two metacompetencies of identity and adaptability to chart a course through the work terrain; together, the metacompetencies give individuals a sense of when it is time to change and the capacity to change. Hall's conceptualization of the protean career, which concentrates on inner psychological variables, finds a complement in Arthur's (1994) conceptualization of the boundaryless career. Rather than stability tied to one firm, an unbound career consists of a sequence of positions characterized by physical and psychological mobility that crosses organizations. Individuals with greater career competencies, including identity and adaptability, may find more opportunities for mobility.

The loss of stable structures and predictable trajectories has led to what has been called the "individualization of the life course" (Beck, 2002). The institutionalized individualism of postmodern life occurred because work no longer spins the axis of life around which other roles revolve. Nonstandard work produces nonstandard lives. Individuals cannot securely identify their place in the world with the work they perform. Individualization of the life course calls for individuals to navigate transitions by using what has been referred to as both *biographicity* (Alheit, 1995) and *identity work* (Sveningsson & Alvesson, 2003). Biographicity denotes the self-referential process by which individuals integrate new and sometimes puzzling experiences into their biographies. Identity work denotes the process of identity construction and revision to cope with the uncertainties provoked by life tasks, transitions, and traumas. It includes the interpretative activities of "forming, repairing, maintaining, strengthening and revising the constructions that are productive of a sense of coherence and distinctiveness" (Sveningsson & Alvesson, 2003, p. 1165). Biographicity and identity work produce identity capital. Although organizations still provide financial capital, individuals must produce their own identity capital by knowing, liking, and using their own story. To assist in producing identity capital, 21st-century career interventions should help individuals construct and use their life stories to make choices and take actions with integrity of character.

A NEW PARADIGM

New theory cannot be just an addition to or extension of the old ideas. The formulation of a new paradigm for career theory must be based in biographicity and identity work, with an accompanying intervention model concentrated on employability, adaptability, emotional intelligence, and lifelong learning. The social reorganization of work in the 21st century requires a fundamental reordering of career theory envisioned from different perspectives and elaborated from new premises. For example, the modern idea of actualizing a core self that already exists within a person served career counseling well during the second half of the 20th century. However, for careers in the 21st century, that idea can be replaced with the postmodern idea that an essential self does not exist a priori; instead, constructing a self is a life project. This view considers self to be a story, not a substance defined by a list of traits.

Needless to state, self-actualization and self-construction offer fundamentally different perspectives on and prospects for career counseling. To be clear, the ideas in this book build on and venerate the contributions of the positivist perspective exemplified by the contributions of Holland's (1997) differential psychology and Super's (1990) developmental psychology, yet they emerge from a constructionist perspective that emphasizes narrative psychology. The traditional theories of Holland and Super are neither true nor false; they substantiate a set of practices constructed to organize the work of vocational guidance and career education. Because of their significance and usefulness, these theories should be sustained. However, traditional theories must also be supplemented by new practices because they cannot be stretched to address the needs of mobile workers in flexible organizations and fluid societies.

Accordingly, career construction theory (Savickas, 2005) responds to the needs of today's mobile workers who may feel anxious and angry as they encounter a restructuring of occupations, transformation of the labor force, and multicultural imperatives. In an uncertain world, developing skills and talents remains important, yet there is no substitute for a grounded sense of self. Thus, career construction theory concentrates on self-construction through work and relationships. Well-being in knowledge societies requires that individuals take possession of their lives by connecting who they are to what they do. To provide counseling to individuals that moves them from finding one's life work to constructing how to make one's life work requires a science of intervention that deals with designing a life and deciding how to use work in that life.

OVERVIEW

Before presenting the model of career counseling, Chapter 2 examines the core concepts of self, identity, meaning, mastery, and mattering. Chapter 3 explains how practitioners use narrative psychology to help clients revise their career stories to increase comprehension, coherence, and continuity. Chapter 4 describes the framework and elements of the career story interview during which practitioners ask story-crafting questions. The next three chapters discuss systematic assessment of the data elicited during a career story interview. Chapter 5 presents the assessment goals that concentrate on extracting client preoccupations and problems from the early recollections that sustain them. Chapter 6 describes how to identify client solutions to the problems they pose in their early recollections. Chapter 7 discusses how to use career themes to extend clients' occupational plots by identifying fitting settings, possible scripts, and future scenarios. Having completed discussion of the career story assessment protocol, the final two chapters concentrate on using the assessment results in career counseling. The penultimate chapter describes how practitioners compose an identity narrative that reconstructs clients' small stories into a large story that encourages reflexivity to clarify choices. The final chapter explains the importance of turning intention to action, first through exploration and trial, then through deciding and doing. The chapter concludes with the case of Raymond to illustrate career construction counseling. A glossary defines specialized words used in the text.

2

Constructing Self and Identity

Career construction theory views making a self as a task. Individuals construct a self by reflecting on experience using the uniquely human capacity to be conscious of consciousness. Self-consciousness, or awareness of awareness, requires language (Neuman & Nave, 2009). Without language, reflection cannot take place, and it is reflexive thinking that builds the self. So language constitutes a critical element in career construction theory because in addition to building a self, it also builds a subjective career. An objective career denotes the sequence of roles an individual occupies from school through retirement. Everyone has an objective career, one that other people may observe across time. However, building a subjective career resembles the task of building a self. A subjective career emerges from thought or mental activity that constructs a story about one's working life. It requires mentation to remember past roles, analyze present roles, and anticipate future roles. Not everyone takes time to reflect on their work lives enough to build a subjective career. And a subjective career cannot be constructed with just awareness of living in the present. It requires self-awareness, especially self-conscious reflection that constructs continuity across the past, present, and future. This reflexive project of personhood requires the use of language.

Career construction theory differs from career theories that consider language as representational. Traditional career theories rest on an epistemology that asserts that language represents and provides a means to express thoughts and feelings that have a prior existence. In comparison, career construction theory rests on the belief that language both constructs and constitutes social realities. Consider this example from a recent memoir (Gorokhova, 2009) about growing up in Leningrad during the 1960s. A 10-year-old girl, in doing her English homework, became puzzled by the word *privacy*. Her tutor explained that there is no Russian word for *privacy*; it simply does not exist. The girl thought it strange that Westerners had something that Russians did not have. As we talk, so we make. Words provide a resource for living that enables thinking and making meaning. As noted previously, career construction theory prefers to concentrate on constructing a self, not actualizing an essential self. Words do not come to adhere to an a priori, essential self. Rather, language provides the words needed to form self-conceptions and constitute a self. The poet Wallace Stevens (1952) explained this elegantly in his poem "The Idea of Order at Key West":[1]

> . . . And when she sang, the sea,
> Whatever self it had, became the self
> That was her song, for she was the maker. Then we,
> As we beheld her striding there alone,
> Knew that there never was a world for her
> Except the one she sang and, singing, made. (p. 131)

Individuals also use language to hold in place the self-awareness emerging from reflexivity. In a sense, we live inside language because language contains the self as words retain the past and anticipate the future. Because language provides the means needed to constitute a self, the lack of a word means a lack of the associated view of self. In counseling for self-

---

[1] Excerpt of "The Idea of Order at Key West" from The Collected Poems of Wallace Stevens by Wallace Stevens, copyright 1954 by Wallace Stevens and renewed 1982 by Holly Stevens. Used by permission of Alfred A. Knopf, a division of Random House, Inc.

construction, practitioners attend closely to a client's language, for those words constitute a client's self and forge a channel along which life may flow (cf. Kelly, 1955). To form new views of self and open novel vistas on the work world, clients may need new words. As they speak new words, they make new worlds. And the new worlds present opportunities to engage in different scenarios and unfamiliar actions.

Although individuals talk their own selves into existence, they need more than language to construct a self. People need experiences on which to reflect, particularly interpersonal experiences, because a self is built from the outside in, not from the inside out. As noted by Vygotsky (1978), "There is nothing in mind that is not first of all in society" (p. 142). Using language as a tool, people coordinate their actions and social relations. So a self is not actually self-constructed, it is coconstructed through active, collaborative processes. We need each other to make sense of ourselves and the world in which we live. In the process of sense making, the idea of self as a separate person arises. Through self-conscious awareness, the self recognizes itself. This self-consciously created idea of a separate self is constituted by stories about experience. In a sense, self-conscious reflection through language is the process that makes a self, and the resulting stories are the content that constitute that self in the form of featured events and favored attributes. In sum, self is an emergent awareness that is culturally shaped, socially constituted, and narrated by language.

IDENTITY

Career construction theory clearly differentiates self from identity. Self is not identity, nor is it absorbed into identity. Self is larger than identity. In the social sciences, identity has many meanings, generally dealing with an individual's understanding of self in society. In career construction theory, identity involves how people think of themselves in relation to social roles. Self-in-role or role identities are socially constructed definitions of self in social situations or environmental contexts. Identity schematizes the self by locating it in a social context (Markus, 1977). The schema called *identity* is a pattern imposed by the individual to mediate and guide his or her response to social realities. Using a syllogism, one could think of identity forming as an individual's thesis (self) encounters the world's antithesis (role) and crafts a synthesis (identity). Thus, identities are coconstructed by a psychological self and a social context. Individuals begin to form psychosocial identities by associating the psychological self with interpersonal experiences and cultural expressions. In due course, individuals consolidate these attributes into a coherent and unified whole, a gestalt that organizes their beliefs, competencies, and interests. Coherence and continuity function to form and develop identity as individuals assemble and integrate these attributes (McAdams & Olson, 2010). Identity crystallizes when individuals join a social group that provides a recognizable social niche. Through this connection to other people, they become identified with community habitats such as neighborhoods, churches, schools, and occupations. The person then pursues purpose and values within their validating and stable communities. From this perspective, occupational choice involves niche construction performed by a self to identify and pursue a work role using socially salient cultural scripts. Occupation provides a way for individuals to flourish in a community.

Being a psychosocial construct, identity resides at the interface of self, context, and culture. The view of identity presented in this volume follows the pattern of Western societies that privilege the individual over the group. The individualistic perspective of Western psychology views self-authorship of identity as a personal project. Nevertheless, MacIntyre (1981) explained that the person narrates the life story yet does not author it alone. Many events and people coauthor the story told by the individual. This view is more compatible with collectivist cultures, in which identity is seldom an individual project. Rather, it is a family project and, often, a community project. In both individualistic and collectivistic communities, individual identity is coconstructed. However, in different cultures and communities, the balance of authority in this collaborative activity may tip toward the self or others. To denote this authorial balance, practitioners may use the terms *chosen* identity and *conferred* identity, yet always remembering that, whether achieved or adopted, identity is fundamentally coconstructed. And from a Western perspective, individuals with conferred identities still make choices about how to enact uniquely their normative identities.

In forming an identity, individuals make choices and commitments. They choose their relationship to the facts of their contexts. In committing to the facticity of their lives, individuals make some emotional compromises with reality and project them forward for some considerable amount of time. In so doing, they take hold of themselves by gripping viscerally certain convictions, and then they cling unflinchingly to these beliefs as they experience confusing and conflicting ideas. Their choices and commitments shape a habitual mode of synchronizing internal needs with external demands. Relative to the work role, declaring an occupational choice states what an individual wants to mean to other people. The choice of an occupational role and commitment to its script crystallizes vocational identity, offers a framework for further decision making, and enhances a sense of agency.

Identity is much more variable than conceptions of the self. Identity commitments do provide a stable significance, at least for some period of time. Nevertheless, identity responds to contexts that evoke different selves, what Holstein and Gubrium (1999) referred to as "geographies of self-making." So identity continuously adapts and changes in negotiating social positions and interpersonal discourses. Accordingly, identity development is a lifelong process. An individual must repeatedly revise identity to adaptively integrate significant new experiences into the ongoing life story.

Developing or revising an identity accelerates when the content of the current identity is insufficient or unable to support the individual in confronting a new set of demands imposed by the society. A story that cannot be completed as planned must be revised. When this occurs, individuals feel anxious because they face challenging situations without the protection of an identity that holds and comforts them. In the domain of work life, this anxiety may be prompted by vocational development tasks, occupational transitions, or work traumas. Developmental tasks and customary transitions may be anticipated and positive, such as completing a training program. In comparison, individuals experience unwanted transitions and unexpected traumas, such as the sudden loss of a job, as negative and even disturbing. Whether perceived as positive or negative, the changes prompted by tasks, transitions, and traumas may acutely disorient individuals and thereby produce confusion, conflict, or contradiction in their meaning system. These feelings signal that a person may be losing a sense of identity.

In the work role, moving without a clear identity may be experienced as career indecision or uncertainty. The initial recognition of dissonance and disequilibrium feels troubling because individuals cannot readily assimilate their experiences into stable and satisfying meaning. At first, individuals repeatedly try to assimilate the dislocation into their existing identity and meaning system. At some point, dissonance rises to the critical threshold at which the individual needs to restore balance through accommodation (Brandtstadter, 2009). Reintegration of identity after its fragmentation and disintegration requires new language and broader discourse. The person must bring the experience into accord with existing schemas by elaborating the current meaning system or creating new meaning. Then the identity work of making sense begins in earnest. This adaptation through accommodation drives development by constructing a more viable sense of identity, one marked by tighter integration and stronger stability.

It is usually the need to accommodate a major vocational development task, significant occupational transition, or serious work trauma that prompts individuals to seek career counseling to further their identity work. Accommodating a series of small yet important problems fosters development because it is easier to restore equilibrium after smaller upsets. The accumulation of several small problems or a single large problem can stall development because it requires more time and effort to accommodate substantial transformations in meaning. When identity gets challenged or problematized, whether by a sum of small tasks or a single substantial task, the current identity may be inadequate to support movement into a new social space. Reworking the identity to accommodate novel or problematic challenges involves narrative processing of identity.

NARRATIVE IDENTITY

Identity is formed by and expressed in narratives (McAdams, 2001). Self-awareness is not apprehended through a list of traits or even in sentences. Self-knowledge resides in stories. Narratives about identity provide understanding in the form of an interpretation of self that orients one to a social world. Through narratives, individuals interpret the self as if they were another person. As William James (1890) famously explained, the "I" tells a story about "me." Similarly, the Danish novelist Isak Dinesen wrote, "To be a person is to have a story to tell" (quoted in Christensen, n.d.). We can only say who we are when we know our own story. These stories about "me" are the substance that individuals process to construct an identity narrative.

Career construction practitioners use the term *narrative identity* to denote a story that an individual tells about the self in some social role or context. In a sense, it is the embodiment of what philosopher Hans-Georg Gadamer (1960/1975) called "the dialogue that we are." McAdams and Olson (2010) defined narrative identity as "an internalized and evolving life story that a person begins to develop in late adolescence to provide life with meaning and purpose" (p. 527). Individuals need to perform narrative identity work when they stop doing a routine and start doing life differently. The challenge of dislocation may be seen as unwanted and unwarranted, or it may be seen as an opportunity to reconstruct the life and start a new story line. Either way, narrative identity work involves an active effort to acknowledge and analyze the impact of a novel experience or a troubling social expectation.

The term *narrative identity* presents an oxymoron—that is, a phrase in which two words of contradictory meaning are used together for special effect. From the Latin *idem,* meaning "the same," *identity* connotes permanence, similarity, and repetition. In comparison, *narrative* connotes change, difference, and alteration. So identity stability opposes narrative fluidity. Thus, "narrative identity" mixes fidelity and flexibility in telling how one changes yet, in some important ways, remains the same. An identity narrative tells a life history that revises identity over time without losing its essential meaning. It tells a story about self, a narrative of becoming oneself in response to the continuous changes that occur during the life course. Narrative processing of identity occurs when individuals feel that they are changing yet do not know who they are becoming. They need to author a narrative identity that sustains sameness yet accounts for change as they reposition themselves in social space. Narrative revision works out the problem of identity sameness to resolve the current dislocation.

In revising a narrative identity, individuals try to grasp the order in their lives through reflection and contemplation. They seek to bridge transitions by using autobiographical reasoning "to keep a story going" (Giddens, 1991, p. 54). Conversational storytelling is the microprocess through which this identity work proceeds as individuals attempt to make sense of self and situation. In the quest to find a way to flourish, they usually learn something that can be incorporated as meaningful change in their life story, a change that brings greater depth, complexity, and wisdom. This change clarifies the world and makes it a little different from the way they had previously seen it. The new learning and the salve of meaning propel the adaptive process that restores balance.

Narrative processing of identity gathers small stories, or *micronarratives*, about important incidents and episodes (Neimeyer & Buchanan-Arvay, 2004). Whereas most small stories deal with everyday events, narrative processing usually focuses on significant figures and important incidents, often involving self-defining moments and life-changing experiences. In working with the micronarratives, the person actively gathers the story threads and weaves them together into one tapestry to craft a unified sense of individuality. Integration of small stories about the self in social situations constructs a large story, or *macronarrative* (Neimeyer & Buchanan-Arvay, 2004). The small stories are memoirs that report particular events more or less objectively. In contrast, the large story resembles an autobiography because it assigns present meaning to past experiences (Weintraub, 1975). Placing the formerly isolated experiences and events into one large story invests them with broader meaning.

The narrative identity processing winnows experiences to make sense and sediment values, attitudes, and habits into a macronarrative that tells a grand story about the life history. The person becomes a character in a world that he or she has constructed. The macronarrative bestows meaning and substance on a life as it tells about pattern and progress. The macronarrative explains our self to our self as it tells how we put the world together. It also explains our self to other people. Telling the life story to other people not only crystallizes what we think of ourselves, it instructs them in how we want them to think about us. Individuals revise the macronarrative as necessary to comprehend and confront the challenges that they currently face—that is, the trouble that a previous version of their life story could not accommodate. Successful narrative identity processing figures out how the individual may move to a new place in the world.

The identity work of narrative processing may also be called *biographical work. Biographicity* means the self-referential ability of individuals to organize and integrate new and sometimes puzzling experiences into their biographies (Alheit, 1995). Practitioners foster biographicity by helping clients view dislocations and interruptions as transitions. The ensuing biographical work considers the impasse, contemplates what is at stake, and clarifies the available choices. To accommodate new experiences and knowledge, the client and practitioner collaborate to rework and transform what the client knows and its meaning. These discussions enhance a sense of biographical agency and encourage the client to plot a story line that bridges the discontinuity (Heinz, 2002). The best accommodation reorganizes the meaning system to tighten integration and strengthen stability. It produces a generative structure that individuals may use to bridge the experiences that initially prompted fragmentation and instability. In the end, the reorganized meaning system manages the transfer from the past to the future. This broader and deeper meaning system increases the biographical agency to deal with the demands of tasks, transitions, and traumas. Thus, counseling reestablishes and elaborates a sense of continuity with which to make transitions without losing self. The client is then able to move forward in a way that simultaneously preserves and transforms the past. The reorganization of a meaning system begins as the client narrates life stories.

CAREER AS STORY

Individuals inscribe their identities with a macronarrative that tells their life story. Storying is the essence of identity work, particularly crafting stories that tell about a gap in life. Stories, or at least the kind in which practitioners are interested, arise in response to the unexpected. Stories try to impose meaning on the unforeseen or inappropriate. If everything goes as expected, there is no need for a story. For example, if you take a trip to the mall and arrive as expected, there is no need for a story. However, if you get lost or have a flat tire, then you have a story. So life stories tell about disruptions in or deviations from the normal, appropriate, expected, or legitimate. They tell how individuals are marked or flawed as well as what they want, lack, or need. These problems and predicaments represent a gap between what should be and what is. They tell of the discrepancy between what people expect from others and what they receive. According to Bruner (1990), people use stories to make sense of these disruptions and deviations.

Occupational Plot

The story tries to explain the variation and fill the gap with meaning. To do so, the individual creates a story to organize events into a sequence, which contributes to their comprehensibility. "Tick" is not a story, yet "tick-tock" is (Kermode, 1966). As the art curator John Baldessari noted, "as soon as you put two things together, you have a story" (quoted in O'Sullivan, 2006, p. 24). However, the sequence of a chronicle that disposes events in the order of time merely terminates. Plotting the sequence of events adds explanations and endings to the experiences that may otherwise still feel random. Plots structure the sequence of events into a coherent whole with a beginning, middle, and end as well as raise some facts to prominence while ignoring others. The end or conclusion brings the narrative closure that a chronicle lacks (White, 1981). E. M. Forster (1927, Chapter 5) explained that a story tells what happened, whereas a plot tells why it happened. He exemplified this difference between story and plot as follows: "The King died, and then the Queen died" is a story because it has a sequence. In comparison, "The King died, and then the Queen died of grief" is a plot because it adds causality. In career construction theory, the sequence of occupational positions in a résumé chronicles an objective career. Each occupation may be viewed as a short story in the novel of career. Then explaining connections and relationships among the occupations "emplots" the objective career and, in so doing, composes a subjective career. *Emplot* simply means assembling elements into a narrative with a plot (Ricoeur, 1984).

In career construction theory, the identity narrative resembles a novel in short stories. The micronarratives constitute the short stories that the individual links to form a long story or macronarrative. The small stories provide possible incidents and episodes that the individual may select in composing a large story. The individual sketches the macronarrative by emplotting the short stories into a narrative identity. Emplotment arranges the separate small stories in a sequence directed toward a conclusion. It uses the small stories to illustrate and corroborate the larger, grand story of a life. Emplotment also configures the diverse incidents and different episodes into a part–whole structure in which the parts gather meaning in relation to the whole. Analogous to musical notes in a melody, the parts are arranged into a whole. Listeners do not hear a melody one note at a time; they experience it as a whole that unites the notes already played, being heard, and expected next. Emplotting a macronarrative makes a life whole because it allows the individual to recognize a pattern. As the microstories accumulate and cohere, they reveal an implicit pattern of recurrence, repetition, and continuity. In the end, the pattern in a life reveals people to themselves and others.

The pattern implicit in the short stories may be thought of as a line that runs through the micronarratives. This *through line* unifies the small stories into a macronarrative by tracing a central line of development through a variegated picture. It is the wire on which the beads of a life story are strung. The through line makes the identity narrative comprehensible because it patterns the small stories. Greek mythology (Graves, 1993) symbolizes the through line as the length of golden thread that guided Theseus back to the outer world through a maze of dark tunnels. Life design counseling, as the reader will learn, concentrates attention on an individual's golden thread. The practitioner wants each client to leave counseling fully capable of appreciating the poem by William Stafford (1999) titled "The Way It Is":[2]

> There is a thread that you follow. It goes among things
> That change. But it doesn't change.
> People wonder about what you are pursuing.
> You have to explain about the thread.

---

[2] Excerpt of William Stafford, "The Way It Is" from *The Way It Is: New and Selected Poems.* Copyright © 1998 by the Estate of Willam Stafford. Reprinted with the permission of Graywolf Press, Minneapolis, Minnesota, www.graywolfpress.org.

But it is hard for others to see.
While you hold it you cannot get lost.
Tragedies happen; people get hurt
or die; and you suffer and get old.
Nothing you can do stops time's unfolding.
You don't ever let go of that thread. (p. 144)

Career Theme

The pattern woven by the golden thread of a through line may be called a *theme*. The golden theme is the controlling idea implicit in the plot. The thematic pattern woven by this central idea provides the primary unit of meaning used to understand the facts of the occupational plot. The career theme provides a unifying idea that, through reoccurrence, makes a life whole. As individuals incorporate new experiences, they use the implicit theme to comprehend the plot episodes by imposing the pattern of meaning on them. When individuals face challenges and disruptions, the recurrent pattern in the macronarrative theme directs action by providing order and overarching goals.

In considering career construction, the theme denotes a moving perspective that imposes personal meaning on past memories, present experiences, and future aspirations. Self-defining stories about the vocational tasks, occupational transitions, and work traumas that an individual has faced from school entry through retirement reveal the essential meaning of career and the dynamics of its construction. Career construction theory, simply stated, holds that individuals build their careers by imposing meaning on vocational behavior. This meaning is held in implicit themes that weave through explicit plots that compose the macronarrative about vocational identity.

Recall that in constructing a narrative identity, individuals work out the problem of their sameness across time. This continuity is represented by a theme that articulates a purposive attitude toward life and states the idea that the life serves. A theme in a macronarrative traces how a person is identical with self despite diversity across micronarratives. Even when everything seems to change, the theme remains the same. Career construction theory concentrates on thematic unity because it carries the motives and meaning that pattern a work life. Similar to motivic development in Viennese classical music, the theme makes a life sing. Beethoven generated the entire score of his Fifth Symphony from a short theme of fate knocking at the door. People listen to that symphony without consciously following the development of the theme through four long movements. Nevertheless, listeners hear the symphony as an integrated and inevitable whole. Recognizing the theme in a narrative identity enables individuals to see self as an integrated and inevitable whole, offering an important way of viewing self and explaining oneself to others.

As in a symphony, there may be multiple thematic threads in a life, with each theme enhancing the other and developing the pattern, the essential characteristic being unity of the life symphony. Given multiple themes, the "unifying self" ontologically conjoins the themes to produce an image of singular purpose. This simplified and self-protective illusion of intrapsychic unity fosters emotional security (Bromberg, 2006). So for counseling, practitioners usually concentrate on a single, dominant career theme, believing that it suffices to comprehend a client's occupational plot and optimizes decision making and problem solving. Additional, major themes may be needed if counseling expands to discuss intimate partnerships or other domains of life. In short, emplotment of client work histories usually relies on a single career theme, or through line, to draw the scenes and episodes together, yet when necessary practitioners may weave multiple themes together into a more layered and complex whole.

When relying on a single theme, not every small story has to follow the through line; some micronarratives may tell about exceptions and complexities within the macronarrative. Identity stories seek some amount of coherence and continuity to maintain a clear and unified story. Yet some lives are complicated, some client themes are more complex than others, and some individuals live multiple plots. So a variegated identity narrative may present multiple themes that are complimentary, confused, conflicted, chaotic, or contradictory. As Walt Whitman (1855/2008) wrote in "Song of Myself",

> Do I contradict myself?
> Very well then I contradict myself
> (I am large, I contain multitudes.) (Stanza 51, Lines 6–8)

Autobiographical reasoning seeks to create some unity, not uniformity, out of contradictory views, baffling behaviors, and inconsistent themes. This unity must be achieved in a properly complicated way that integrates diversity without homogenizing it. Rather than the metaphor of a symphony, these complex individuals better fit the metaphor of jazz that improvises on a theme from diverse angles. It completes the whole through arrangements that reveal the shape beneath the surface and highlight the harmony among dissonant stories.

The theme, clear or complicated, carries to work settings the concerns that constitute the individual and matter most in defining self and expressing identity. This makes work the outer form of something intensely personal. In career construction theory, the theme is what matters in the life story. It consists of what is at stake in that person's life. And it matters both to the individual and to other people. On the one hand, the theme matters to individuals in that it gives meaning and purpose to their work. It makes them care about what they do. On the other hand, what they do and contribute to society matters to other people. The belief that what they do matters to others sharpens identity and promotes a sense of social attachment. What matters most forms a horizon of values that individuals use to evaluate experience. Values name the constitutive concerns that make the identity narrative an ethical and aesthetic project because they connect the individual to a broader reality or greater story. The pattern of higher meaning can be expressed as universal values such as the themes of strength, knowledge, beauty, equality, service, relationships, and justice. This pattern of higher meaning is not the moral of the story; it is the thematic purpose pursued in the occupational plot.

Objective Versus Subjective Career

Some writers equate theme and plot. I do not. I consider plot and theme as two perspectives on a narrative identity. An identity narrative includes both a concrete plot and an abstract theme about the journey through life. Journey poses as a metaphor for the process that underlies all growth, learning, and self-discovery. The explicit plot concerns the *outer journey* as it tells about dramatic events, crisis points, life-defining moments, and coordinated action toward certain goals. The plot tells about the quest to reach certain goals and elaborate the self in social context. In comparison, the implicit theme concerns the *inner journey* as it tells about an emotional odyssey shaped by a central conflict with its associated needs and longings. The underlying and implicit theme adds meaning and purpose to the plot of the macronarrative. Although it tells of emotional transformations, it is more timeless and abstract than the plot.

Career construction theory views career as a story, or the sequence of positions that an individual occupies. An occupational plot pulls the sequence of positions together as episodes in an objective career, one publicly observable and recorded. The personal theme provides coherence and continuity in making a subjective career, one privately experienced. Although both plot and theme may be considered career, the first objective and the second subjective, career construction theory refers to the objective career as occupational plot and the subjective career as career theme. Objective outcomes such as success or failure are part of the occupational plot, whereas subjective outcomes such as satisfaction or frustration are part of the career theme. In sum, a story describes what happened, the plot tells why it happened, and the theme explains what it means.

Character Arc

The career theme carries the character arc or overarching narrative thread. *Arc* is a contraction of *overarching*. It does not mean that the thematic line must have a certain shape such as rising tension followed by resolution. The arc could be a straight line, showing repetition without resolution. The essential point is that the character arc extends through the entire macronarrative, telling the status of the individual's primary motivation and major impetus as it unfolds. The character arc portrays where the individual started, is now, and wants to end up on some essential issue. The character arc begins with an impetus that moves the individual. Typically it is about something missing in life, something that individuals need or for which they long. To overcome this limitation or weakness, they seek to attain goals that fulfill the need. They try to fix the flaw that begins the identity narrative. As they move from inner darkness toward outer light, they wrestle with the fear, limitation, block, or wound. In due course, they learn how to overcome the adversity and transcend their flaws as they become something more than they were.

The progress from need to goal transforms individuals as they grow, develop, and learn. For example, fear becomes courage or loneliness becomes relationships. Oprah Winfrey said, "I grew up a little Negro child who felt so unloved and isolated—the emotion I felt most as a child was loneliness—and now the exact opposite has occurred for me in adulthood" (quoted in McAdams, 2008, p. 23). However, loneliness does not have to resolve in relationships; it just has to be solved. The cult film director John Waters (2006) said he went from feeling lonely to learning to be alone. The transformation of need into goal also explains the old saying that your greatest strength is also your greatest weakness. This transformation represents the core of the character—that is, the character arc that defines the person and explains the driving force of the plot.

In listening to clients' small stories, practitioners must have a way in which to focus concentration. Otherwise, they cannot reconstruct the collection of short stories into a theme with a character arc. A systematic approach to listening and making sense of client micronarratives requires a paradigm. Just as the sonata form can organize musical thought, career construction practitioners need a form to organize client stories. A theory of texts provides this pattern as it organizes close listening to certain elements of the micronarratives. Literary criticism offers various theories for the close reading needed to understand stories. Bressler (2006) explained 11 major theories of literary criticism that could be useful in listening for how stories construct career, including the mythic (Jungian), psychoanalytic (Freudian), structural (systemic), poststructural (deconstruction), Marxist (economic), and feminist (cultural). Each of these theories directs attention to different elements of a story based on preconceived expectations and strategies for understanding. These reading strategies form a frame of reference that produces meaning from a narrative. The reading strategy for career construction counseling is called the *narrative para-*

digm. Although the narrative paradigm seems highly effective, practitioners acknowledge that the strategy provides only a partial and positional perspective.

A NARRATIVE PARADIGM

To deal directly with client stories from the theoretical perspective of career construction, practitioners apply a narrative paradigm to organize the client's biographical stories. *Narrative* denotes a story, and *paradigm* denotes a pattern or model. So *narrative paradigm* refers to a mode of understanding or a pattern that practitioners apply to client microstories to identify a character arc in the macronarrative. The narrative paradigm is essentially an integrative conceptual framework for synthesizing a particular understanding of a macronarrative about identity.

The narrative paradigm rests on a single principle for making connections among the client's experiences, expectations, and explanations. This psychological principle was articulated by the Canadian philosopher Charles Taylor (1992): "We must inescapably understand our lives in narrative forms as a quest" (p. 520). The quest involves filling a hole in the heart by prevailing over trials and tribulations. Adversity provides the tension that propels the quest. The client's view of adversity forms the essential organizing principle in the drama. Viewing life as a quest is inherent in many theories of psychotherapy. For example, Adler (1956) portrayed an individual's "line of movement" or *life line* as proceeding from a felt negative to a perceived plus; Viktor Frankl (1963) wrote that as individuals turn their predicaments into achievements, they move from tragedy to triumph; and Jungian analysts believe that individuation involves moving from misery to meaning (Hollis, 1993). Individuals reach out to the environment toward self-forming and self-fulfilling solutions to problems in growing up. They gather from the real world those materials and resources that they use to develop themselves and pursue their life projects. In addition to Adler's construct of life line, numerous other through lines or life theme constructs play a central role in personality theories, including Allport's (1961) proprium, Berne's (1972) script, Erikson's (1968) ego identity, Kelly's (1955) core role, Lecky's (1945) self-consistency, McAdam's (2008) redemptive self, Murray's (1938) unity theme, Reich's (1933) character, and Sartre's (1943) project. Csikszentmihalyi and Beattie (1979) offered the clearest explanation of a character arc in the thematic movement through life: "A life theme consists of a problem or set of problems which a person wishes to solve above everything else and the means the person finds to achieve a solution" (p. 48). So career construction theory relies on the idea that people organize their lives around a problem that preoccupies them and a solution that occupies them.

Life themes originate early in childhood as unfinished situations and incompletely formed gestalt. In this sense, themes carry a yearning to fill the gap or complete the story. They linguistically portray environmental limitations, disruptive events, and personal deficiencies that the individual intends to overcome and transcend. As an easily activated cognitive scheme, the person uses it to search for a potential benefit in the environment. A prime example for career construction theory is that individuals seek work they may use to move toward the progressive realization of wholeness. The character arc reveals the transformations that have occurred during the individual's progressive self-cultivation of wholeness. The character arc is anchored by the problem that the individual wishes to solve above all others, the core of the theme and its preoccupation. As Bruce Springsteen explained to *60 Minutes* interviewer Scott Pelley (2007), "Every good writer or filmmaker has something eating at them that they can't quite get off their back. And so your job is to make your audience care about your obsession." Or as Hans Christian Andersen wrote to Henriette Collin, "I have to make something of the torments that are inflicted on me" (quoted in Simon, 2005). Or as more simply stated in Andersen's (1872/2008) final story, "Auntie Toothache," "A great poet must have a great toothache" (Part IV, Stanza 27). Whether obsession or toothache causes the pain, reducing the hurt becomes an overarching goal in the life quest. As the American psychologist William James wrote in his diary, to prevail over their trials and tribulations people must "ascend to some sort of partnership with fate and since tragedy is at the heart of us, go meet it, work it in to your own ends instead of dodging it all your days" (quoted in Barzun, 1983, p. 19).

The most powerful statement of the line of movement from passive to active appears in *Paradise Lost* when Milton (1940/1667) described how Lucifer, upon arriving in Hell, announced to his followers, "Our torments also may, in length of time, become our elements" (p. 33). To me this sentence means that by transcending their trials and tribulations, people transform themselves into the opposite. As already noted, fear becomes courage and loneliness becomes relationships. An individual's strongest capabilities emerge from the solutions to the problems he or she has resolved. Freud (1953) conveyed this idea as a basic tenet of his theory: "Where id was, there ego shall be" (p. 80), or where the problem was, I must become. In moving from victim to victor, the individual turns tension to intention, preoccupation to occupation, obsession to profession, negative to positive, weakness to strength, and lemons to lemonade. People convert symptom into strength through actively mastering what they passively suffered. This explains how a boy with a speech impediment became the Greek orator Demosthenes (Worthington, 2001) and how after being bullied by others, the scrawny weakling named Angelo Siciliano became the bodybuilder known as Charles Atlas (McCarthy, 2007).

Repetition aimed at mastery composes the life theme. Freud (1948) explained that a repetition compulsion forms the character arc (p. 18). This compulsion to symbolically repeat and relive negative experiences represents an effort to undo or master past adversity by converting it into its opposite or at least getting over it, getting used to it, or learning to live with it. As Peter Pan explained in the first line of the 1953 Disney movie, "All of this has happened before, and it is happening again" (Disney & Luske, 1953). Freud (1948) viewed repetition with mastery as growth and repetition without mastery as neurosis. Each time individuals repeat the issue, they deal with it more effectively and thereby increase stability and integration. Of course, repetition without mastery becomes mental illness, as stated in a definition of insanity often attributed to Albert Einstein: "doing the same thing over and over again and expecting different results." Our lives depend upon which way we unfold our story, repetition with or without mastery.

Career construction chooses to use the narrative paradigm, meaning that practitioners listen to client stories to hear the turn of events during which clients actively master what they have passively suffered. Listening to stories to learn how an individual proposes to turn tension into intention enables practitioners to identify the thematic character arc that reveals how preoccupation becomes occupation. The career theme is central to meaning making. The occupational plot alone is insufficient for career counseling because it essentially portrays a sequence of related episodes without the inner unity of a theme. Occupational plot tells of activity without personal meaning. It portrays the self as agent, not author. To recognize meaning, practitioners use a hermeneutic practice as they search for a theme that grounds the here and now in the there and then. A main way of knowing a part is recognizing that it is part of something. Thus, practitioners discern meaning through a circular interplay between occupational plot and career theme that relates the particulars of a plot episode to a general theme and then back to that particular episode or on to another episode. In career construction theory, this movement from concrete to abstract to concrete progressively settles into a good fit that balances plot and theme. A sense of unity crystallizes as the theme invests plot parts with deeper meaning through their participation in the whole. In the end, the implicit repetition of the theme throughout the plot becomes more explicit.

Throughout this hermeneutic practice of sense making, practitioners resist the temptation of imposing on a client's occupational plot a ready-made theme, such as those provided by Holland's (1997) typology (i.e., Realistic, Investigative, Artistic, Social, Enterprising, and Conventional). Constructionist practitioners descend into details of the story, whereas positivist practitioners rise to abstractions such as types and traits. The thematic pattern of higher meaning recognized through the dialectic between scenes and theme produces a narrative truth from the facts in the plot. Thus, the subjective career theme that guides, regulates, and sustains vocational behavior emerges from an active process of making truths, not discovering preexisting facts. The practitioner wants to hear today's stories, not exhume buried memories. The word *narrative* indicates an account of prior experiences from a present perspective rather than an objective report of past events. A narrative truth may not be an accurate report of fixed facts because the theme repeatedly *re-members*—that is, reinterprets and reconstructs—the past to meet the needs of the next scenario. The theme functions to carry trends from the past steadily forward through the present and into the future. Thus, autobiographical reasoning uses the theme to choose, organize, and present an identity narrative with contemporary meaning and usefulness. The theme provides structure and stricture for making a claim on experience and for re-membering facts into personal meaning and narrative truth. The truthfulness of a narrative then rests on its usefulness in positioning individuals for further experience. From a pragmatic perspective, narrative truth charts a path through reality that fits an individual's pursuit of purpose. In the end, narrative truth is real if it is real in its consequences.

Recognizing narrative truths through a thematic analysis of the past serves as a prologue to resolving the occupational plot problems that clients bring to consultation. Some circumstance has dislocated their occupational plot from its career theme, so they need to reunite plot and theme in a way that imposes order on confusion, conflict, or chaos. The actual intervention involves rebalancing the occupational plot and career theme. Patterning the plot problem with thematic continuity achieves a new equilibrium, one balanced on narrative truth that opens pathways not previously perceived or possible. The more integrative equilibrium enables clients to carry forward their life project more consciously. Then through narrative inventions discussed in the next chapter, practitioners will use this truth to help clients deepen self-understanding of the unfolding plot and strengthen intentionality in shaping the next scenario. The interventions of narrative counseling are presented in the next chapter.

3

Narrative Counseling

Today's mobile workers may feel fragmented and confused by the restructuring of occupations and transformation of the labor force. As they move from one assignment to the next assignment, they must let go of what they did but not who they are. If they let go of everything, then the loss may overwhelm them. By holding onto the self in the form of a life story that provides meaning and continuity, they are able to move on in a way that advances life purpose and approaches overarching goals. As the physician–poet William Carlos Williams explained, "Their story, yours and mine—it's what we all carry with us on this trip that we take" (quoted in Coles, 1989, p. 30). Stories hold in place life lessons that have been learned, and the lessons lead the way through ambiguity by creating scenarios that link future initiatives to past achievements.

Practitioners of career construction counseling use narrative psychology (Crossley, 2000) to help clients unfold their stories, so that in the end the stories can enfold them and quell their uncertainty. Their narrative construction of identity and subjective career provides meaning and direction as they encounter transitions that involve a loss of position, project, and place. Career themes weave a holding environment that sustains meaning, contains anxiety, and secures a space for exploration. To the extent that the career theme holds people, they can master developmental tasks, make vocational transitions, and mitigate occupational traumas.

The life story allows individuals to meet the uncertainties of transition with comforts recalled from the past. It enables clients to appreciate, or at least understand, chaos and disorder as necessary precursors to change, the next chapter. The story orients an individual to new events and absorbs these experiences into the meaning system. This allows individuals to understand their experiences and then make choices about how to proceed. A good story about the self encourages a client to make career changes while holding onto a self that is even more vital and intentional. Thus, most practitioners encourage clients to narrate their stories.

Constructionist counseling is a relationship in which a career is coconstructed through narration. Stories serve as the construction tools for building narrative identity and highlighting career themes in complex social interactions. As they tell their stories, clients feel that the stories become more real. The more stories they tell, the more real they become. The more they view their "me," the more they develop their self-concepts. Storytelling crystallizes what clients think of themselves. Many clients laugh and cry while telling their stories because they hear their life themes emerge in the space between client and practitioner. It is important that practitioners help clients understand the implications of what they have said in telling their stories. This means relating the career theme to the problems posed at the beginning of the first interview. It is also advisable to use clients' most dramatic metaphors and their repeated words. At the same time, practitioners increase and elaborate the language that a client has available to make meaning out of experience. Career counseling may offer clients the logical language of personality types and occupational titles (e.g., Holland, 1997) as well as the dramatic language of cultural narratives and the symbolic language of poetry. Helping clients to enlarge their vocabulary of self increases their ability to story their own experiences, understand who they are, and communicate what they seek. Narrating the self increases comprehension, coherence, and continuity.

COMPREHENSION

Practitioners help clients to know their minds by encouraging them to speak their minds, to narrate their experience. In this sense, self-construction occurs through self-expression, especially when individuals express self within the container of a story. Narration of one's autobiography within a resourceful dialogue increases the intelligibility of the story. At the beginning of counseling, a few clients are strangers in their own lives. Other clients have a glancing relationship with their own lives. Even clients with keen self-knowledge tell stories about themselves that they do not quite understand. Telling the story brings to conscious awareness what already exists, yet it may be obscure and ambiguous. As clients speak what they know, they find that they do not know it as well as they thought. This realization prompts them to learn more about themselves. People make sense of life by articulating it. They grasp their lives in stories. Narration helps clients to produce their own truths as they articulate them. They do not discover meaning and purpose; instead, they create meaning with a point of view that reduces the gap between experience and explanation. In telling their stories, clients come into closer contact with their own life experiences. Furthermore, telling the stories transforms facts into truths and makes that meaning evident to both client and practitioner. Individuals become fuller beings by comprehending what moves them, what they built their lives around, and what ideas their lives serve.

To increase intelligibility, clients make their stories clearer and more convincing. Stories become easier to follow when clients make implicit meanings more evident. Adding details makes the stories more convincing. Specific details make the story more plausible and the teller more certain. Good listeners improve the intelligibility of client stories by asking questions to clarify points. Sometimes listeners may ask for examples, explanations, and evidence that verify and substantiate a story. In addition to increasing comprehension, narrating one's life story gives it more substance. The more people tell their life story, the more real it becomes, and consequently the more real they become.

COHERENCE

Narration can articulate various versions of the self in the context of career. When clients begin to teach practitioners about their lives, the stories start out jumbled. As clients tell their stories, they may report chronicles of the self that, when compared, may be contradictory and inconsistent. Although each micronarrative may be intelligible, two or more small stories may conflict rather than cohere. Inexperienced practitioners may become confused and uncertain when this occurs. In comparison, veteran practitioners become energized because they have found an entry into deeper meaning. Contradictory stories are both "true" and coexist within the client, so determining how they fit together prompts significant progress in sense making and counseling. Through continued narration the stories increasingly fit together, thereby tightening self-consistency (Lecky, 1945) and strengthening integrity. Coherence forms as links join and hold together. To help clients fit stories together, practitioners use connection and repetition as cohesive devices. In due course, clients' chronicles of the self cohere in a way that unifies their identity narrative. Narrative coherence provides a unity in diversity that increases the goodness of the story. A macronarrative configuration, with coherently integrated microstories, enables stronger maintenance of meaning when disruptive events occur.

However, with a few clients, the goal may be to reduce coherence. Occasionally, clients begin counseling with a circumscribed identity that is overly coherent because they equate themselves with a partisan position in a faction, cause, or idea. However, these uncomplicated identities may substantiate an ideology that provides only a partial and temporary positioning. To portray a more dialogic portrait of identity, practitioners increase the complexity of client stories by locating the narrated self in different contexts and roles. Meaning resides within some context of use, not in correspondence to some fixed fact or external reality. So moving the story into different contexts or time periods raises salient issues and highlights different dimensions of identity.

CONTINUITY

Whereas coherence provides stronger maintenance of meaning, continuity provides longer maintenance of meaning. Coherence enhances unity, whereas continuity enhances stability. Clients create continuity in their life stories through narration that reveals secrets, recognizes themes, and retells personal myths. As individuals tell their stories, a theme emerges, and the life starts to make more sense. Story by story, clients strengthen the strands of meaning in the larger narrative, the macronarrative of identity. Gradually, they begin to apprehend and consolidate narrative lines as they recognize the repetition of themes and, in due course, identify the underlying logic of the progression. The process deepens when they discuss their personal secrets. Counseling provides a safe place in which ancient secrets may rise to the surface and forgotten histories emerge from the shadows. Often these secrets reveal the glue that integrates separate stories to create a unified whole. Discussion of secrets also leads to an examination of personal myths that clients repeat to themselves to make sense of the world and to renew their purpose.

NARRATIVE COUNSELING FOR
CAREER CONSTRUCTION

The value of increasing comprehension, coherence, and continuity is assumed by practitioners of narrative counseling. In fact, these narrative elements serve as goals that structure the microprocesses in career counseling. Counseling involves a relational, conversational encounter during which learning and growth occur through storytelling. When people seek career counseling, they have a story to tell. They bring old stories to counseling, and they want to compose a new story with the practitioner. The dialogue helps people examine more than what they like; it helps them to evaluate what they are like. It does so by having clients study their lives in depth, in progress, and in narrative. Career counseling does more than give voice to client stories; it accesses different meanings to open up possibilities and restart stalled initiatives. It seeks a transformative effect that enables a more complete and whole individual to emerge. When storytelling is approached as a transformational process, essential elements of a life are distilled and then felt, explored, and integrated.

Constructionist career counseling emphasizes *mattering* rather than congruence. Mattering confers meaning and substance on people's lives by relating their stories to some pattern of higher meaning such as peace, justice, equality, and beauty. In addition to explicating the meaning and mattering of past experiences, career counseling forges links to the world that lies ahead by promoting intention and action. Having people practice their purpose informs their imagination with new ideas that stir intuition and reveal intentions. Rehearsing purpose fosters the expressive freedom to design a life plan that revitalizes the individual. It always involves considering what work can do for them as well as what work they might do. Whereas mattering brings client experience forward, activity starts clients living ahead of themselves. Career counseling increases the authority that people have in their own lives. Although career counseling involves brief treatment, sometimes a single meeting, it assists clients in more fully inhabiting their lives and becoming more complete as they sustain themselves and contribute to their communities.

Career construction counselors usually follow a standard agenda of dialogue and deliberation, if it suits the client's needs. Similar to a three-act drama, career counseling has three parts. The three parts may be portions of a single interview or three separate interviews. In a three-part drama, the first act introduces the character. In career construction counseling, the first act is the career story interview (see the Appendix), which introduces clients to their practitioners and eventually to themselves. In a drama, the second act presents the essential conflict and ends with a profound understanding that prompts a moment of truth. In career construction counseling, the second act involves presenting and discussing a client's life portrait. New understandings emerge when comparing the portrait to the reason for seeking counseling. The third act in a drama displays the changes prompted by new understanding. In career construction, this is the counseling portion that seeks to resolve the concern the client brought to counseling by revising the client's identity narrative and reorienting his or her career. As Wittgenstein (1953, aphorism 109) observed, "problems are solved, not by giving new information, but by arranging what we always have known since long." In short, during the first act clients *construct* their careers through short stories, during the second act practitioners *reconstruct* the small stories into a large story, and during the third act client and practitioner *coconstruct* a revised identity narrative, new intentions, and possible actions.

COUNSELING MODEL

Similar to other forms of counseling, career construction counseling has two major dimensions: a relationship dimension and a communication dimension.

Relationship Dimension

The relationship between client and practitioner should involve engagement, interaction, and encouragement.

Engagement

Engagement begins when clients have a need that propels them into counseling. The imminent end of a previous adaptation dislocates clients from a life space and occupational plot. This disequilibrium moves them to consult a practitioner. Initially, practitioners must reach out to clients to form a partnership, a working alliance (Masdonati, Massoudi, & Rossier, 2009). Practitioners begin to create this bond by being receptive to who clients are and by welcoming them in the consulting room. To do this, practitioners attend to a client's every word and gesture and, as appropriate, resonate emotionally to these communications. In this narrative approach, practitioners cultivate the relationship as engaged curiosity about clients' career stories.

Interaction

Interaction furthers the working alliance as practitioners first elicit client stories and then provide new perspectives. Eliciting stories, exploring their meaning, and evoking accompanying feelings are elements of narrative craft. The practitioner's job is to attend, listen, and validate the story and its authenticity. Practitioners strive to appreciate the story, not control the interaction. Getting absorbed in a client's story helps the client to relax. So practitioners must join the story, accompanying clients as they narrate their thoughts and feelings. Practitioners connect to client stories by listening to words and phrases and then echoing them with interest. They also prompt clients to elaborate stories by being both in awe and in doubt. They smooth the emotional flow and feel the fullness of the emotions expressed. In addition to attending to client feelings, practitioners must also attend to how they themselves are responding emotionally to client stories.

After listening to some stories, practitioners help clients to begin shaping their macronarrative by both highlighting thematic patterns and processing the dominant affect. To do this, practitioners engage in a highly responsive conversation during which they prompt clients to consider what their stories mean relative to their current dilemma. They use different verbal strategies for examining the meaning of stories than for eliciting client stories. For example, they may use ambiguity to broaden the conversation and loosen meaning. At other times, they may use repetition to narrow the conversation and tighten meaning.

What clients do not say may be quite important. Occasionally, an important part of the life story is not forthcoming. Sometimes clients have a story that cannot be told or that they are not ready to tell. If practitioners sense that something is missing, they may search for the absent material, often by wondering aloud based on emotional resonance. In these instances, practitioners must be sensitive to speak to clients only about material that clients are ready to hear. In all instances, practitioners avoid detached interrogation. They serve as witnesses, not act as detectives. In this regard, I appreciate an analogy to the quintessential detective, Sherlock Holmes. The client resembles Holmes in being a brilliant investigator. The practitioner resembles Dr. Watson in being a confidant who serves to reveal inner thoughts by continually asking Holmes, "How did you figure that out?" and "What does that mean?"

Encouragement

After coming to some understanding of the client's stories and situ.
practitioners add encouraging statements to their empathic respons.
Empathic responses prompt deeper self-exploration as the practitioner
actively listens to the client's perspective by restating and accentuating the
feeling and meaning in client statements. In comparison, encouragement
is a response from the practitioner's perspective. When practitioners speak
from their own vantage point, they seek to help clients consider other perspectives and possibilities. The gift of the practitioner as another perspective is an otherness that requires clients to enlarge themselves and their
stories in some way. This enlargement may require progressive destabiliza-
tions and new equilibriums that move toward change and choice. Practitioners must structure the move toward these commitments in progressive
steps that build momentum and confidence. This structure supports purposeful action that moves a client from the currently experienced situation
to the currently desired situation (Tiedeman & Field, 1962). To promote
client activity both within and beyond the consultation, practitioners build
client courage with statements that concentrate on the required purposeful action. The desired actions are behaviors ripe with meaning. The action
itself marks the key outcome of the consultation and narration. Although
central to narrative therapy, words alone are necessary yet not sufficient.
Words culminate in understanding and preference; actual choice and
change require that clients enact the new meanings of their revised identity
in the real world.

Communication Dimension

The content dimension of career construction counseling consists of stories
and their meaning. Thus, counseling begins with a career story interview
that poses questions to clients so that they may listen to their own lives speak
and, in due course, see themselves in their stories. As a tool for eliciting stories, the structured interview is intended to help clients ask better questions
of themselves. The questions provide a conversational map that practitioners use to invite clients to voice their experience. The interview prompts

clients to unfold their lives by elaborating self-defining experiences. The questions elicit the very narratives that clients are reworking to provide deeper or new meaning for their lives. These self-defining stories describe what matters to clients. The stories reveal life goals that clients think will make them more complete and the problem-solving strategies that serve as a means to achieving those goals. In addition to revealing life themes, stories told during a career story interview also manifest the client's self-constructing type and career adaptability repertoire (Savickas, 2005).

Structure

The application of the career story interview in career construction counseling provides a structured approach intended to be process directive, yet not content directive (Neimeyer, 2004a). Nevertheless, the framework does influence the content by selecting what will be told. The framework serves as a method for practitioners to find their way into the private lives of their clients by organizing the process of self-narration. The strategy presents clients with structured opportunities for experiential self-exploration and personal discovery. This strategy serves primarily to help clients focus their exploring. To meet the needs of each client, practitioners must remain flexible in adopting or dropping the framework. The strategy should never be reduced to a recipe to control the conversation. Instead, the strategy functions to control the practitioner's own anxiety. Because the career story interview questions provide both a process outline for the dialogue and a framework for close listening, the questions offer practitioners a sense of security with which they may approach new clients who will tell unique stories.

The career construction model and interview method direct practitioners to follow the advice of the novelist Eudora Welty (1983)—listen *for* a story rather than listen *to* a story. Listening *to* a story means absorbing it by being passive and receptive. Listening *for* a story means actively discerning it and collaboratively shaping it. This discernment involves listening, at least, for choices made, key concepts, and thematic ideas. In hearing client micronarratives, career construction practitioners listen for the occupation plot, career theme, and character arc.

In listening for the larger story, practitioners use five major questions to orient themselves to the endless amount of biographical details and small stories that a client may narrate. The questions provide practitioners with what Schultz (2002) called a method for "generating psychobiographical hypotheses." The five questions give practitioners something specific to work with—salient memories, self-defining moments, and nuclear scenes. The questions focus clients' narration on the small stories that practitioners use to help clients compose a large story that comprehends their identity and adaptability.

Dialogue

Career construction practitioners agree with Henry James (1908), who wrote that "the teller of a story is primarily, none the less, the listener to it, the reader of it too" (p. viii). Comprehension of clients' own narrative identities emerges from dialogue, not insight. Responding to the interview questions enables clients to hear their own stories in community. The conversational encounter, with its resourceful dialogue and close listening, has clients ask questions of their lives. As clients tell their stories, practitioners prompt clients to elaborate their feelings, beliefs, and goals. The questions direct clients to consider what their experiences mean for self and identity. Practitioners reflect those episodes in the stories that express both the client's change and constancy over time. These reflections and restatements highlight the logic of a client's life and foster meaning making.

Of course, practitioners respond to more than clients' thoughts and stories. They also process affective experiences and respond empathically to present feelings. Practitioners help clients come to terms with how transitions feel to them as they prepare to enter a new story. They draw attention to the story that may be ending and, when appropriate, help clients grieve that loss. In short, practitioners use these conversational strategies to increase the comprehensibility, coherence, and continuity of identity narratives by extending the occupational plot and clarifying the career theme. They aim to further substantiate the self, reorganize identity, and increase self-directedness. Ultimately, practitioners strive to encourage clients to more fully inhabit their own lives and become more completely who they are already. In the words of the Spanish poet Antonio Machado (2003, p. 6) they must realize that they themselves are the way forward:[1]

> Traveller, there is no road,
> You make your own path as you walk.
> As you walk, you make your own road,
> and when you look back
> you see the path.

Listening in a systematic way for the meaning of client micronarratives enables practitioners to recognize a thematic unity that organizes clients' narrative identities. In hearing client responses to the five questions, practitioners listen for the spine of narrative logic that organizes a life. While listening to an individual's career stories to discern and understand the life theme, practitioners may easily become disoriented by the numerous particulars of a life. To prevent becoming confused by a client's complexities and contradictions, practitioners should listen not for the facts but for the glue that holds the facts together as they try to learn the theme that makes a life whole.

Reflection

The seemingly random actions and incidents reported in microstories may be arranged into an occupational plot and career theme in many ways. Career construction theory proposes for this purpose that the listener winnow the quintessence of client stories. Practitioners and researchers do so by assuming that the archetypal theme of career construction involves turning a personal preoccupation into a public occupation. As clients narrate their stories, practitioners concentrate on identifying and understanding the client's personal paradigm for turning need into goal, tension into intention, and obsession into profession. The 20th-century progress narrative about career as climbing the occupational ladder is thus transformed into a progress narrative about using work to actively master what clients have pas-

---

[1] From "xxix" in *There is no road: Proverbs of Antonio Machado* (p. 6), by A. Machado, translated by M. Berg and D. Maloney, 2003, Buffalo, NY: White Pine Press. Copyright 2003 by White Pine Press. Reprinted with permission.

sively suffered. After collecting micronarratives, practitioners may arrange them in a progress narrative that includes hypotheses about the character arc. This procedure enables practitioners to craft from client stories an identity narrative with coherence and continuity. Eventually, practitioner and client engage these hypotheses in an iterative, hermeneutic process to coconstruct a mutual understanding that fully addresses the client's reasons for seeking counseling.

Reflecting on and retelling their stories to a confidant encourages clients to understand how they can use work to become more whole and participate fully in an occupational role that matters both to them and their community. Furthermore, practitioners help clients to increase the narratability of their stories and to relate their career themes to the decisions that they must make and choices they must take. Difficult choices make them clarify their lives. Discussing the alternative choices available to the client and how each one might advance the client's story, the practitioner retells the story in a manner designed to consider what is at stake, increase the client's career adaptability, and identify occupations that can be used to write the next chapter in the client's story. When arranged by the practitioner for retelling, the responses build a scaffold of the known small stories around a knowable large story. The scaffold organizes the meaning space to enable reflection and autobiographical reasoning. After the identity narrative stabilizes to stand alone, the scaffold of small stories around a client's macronarrative may be removed.

CLIENT GOALS

In any counseling relationship, practitioners must help clients find a way to deal with what they feel they must. So practitioners begin by asking clients to articulate and elaborate what they seek from the experience of counseling. Practitioners may do this by asking a client, "How can I be useful to you as you construct your career?" This purposely open question prompts clients to tell important information, much more important than demographic details and historical facts. An individual's response to this opening question enables practitioners to observe a client's style of self-presentation, emotional tone, and way of relating to others. After working with dozens of clients, practitioners become expert at noting client uniqueness. Even clients with similar concerns and self-constructing strategies vary in emphasis, expression, and emotion as they state their goals for consultation.

In using this opening question, practitioners assume responsibility for initiating the relationship by fostering thinking about goals, and they do so in a way that models the mutuality at the center of the relationship. Effective practitioners do not impose goals on clients. Instead, the opening question elicits clients' goals and expectations. Practitioners want to learn the problem that brought a client to counseling and how he or she views that problem. Of course, they need to know where the client wants to go with the problem. And practitioners must learn what the client wants from the consultation and how he or she wants it delivered (Neimeyer, 2004b). If clients state the treatment they want, such as "I want to take an interest inventory," then practitioners probe further to learn what the client wishes to accomplish through that intervention. Practitioners do not want clients to prescribe the intervention; they want to know the client's problems and goals.

Practitioners vary in the amount of background information that they seek in the beginning of a consultation. Some practitioners make few inquiries about history, believing that what they need to know is happening in the moment. Other practitioners make numerous inquiries about the client's history, believing that is important in understanding what is happening in the moment. Most practitioners prefer to let the history unfold as needed for clients to tell their career stories. So, they typically get some context by asking one or two questions about the problem's backstory.

After learning a suitable amount of the backstory, practitioners must concentrate on the client's response to the opening question. Although succinct, a world of information may be prefigured in the sentences that clients use to present their problems. Clients know much more than they can say as they begin counseling. Their response to the opening question may tell a story about themselves that they do not yet quite understand. For many clients, what they know already and what they think they might do about their career concern is implicit in their opening response. Some clients know explicitly from the beginning what they want to do and sometimes even how they want to do it. So, practitioners carefully consider a new client's response to the question of how counseling may be useful. They want to hear if the client may be implicitly stating a solution that she or he already has in mind. As T. S. Eliot (1963) wrote in Four Quartets, the ending is already implicit in the beginning. Part of the process of counseling is to have clients elaborate and narrate that solution so they themselves hear what they want to do next.

The practitioner's job is to amplify what clients say by helping them hear it from different perspectives as they respond to the career story interview questions and later by repeating it several times in coconstructing the client's identity narrative. As the known is spoken, clients hear themselves articulate their own answer to the question they have posed to the practitioner. So clients' explanation of how they think counseling might be useful to them often lays the groundwork for the larger story. The client's response to this opening question sets the agenda for the session and frames the ensuing dialogue. The opening sentence tells practitioners what the story will be about. It directs the practitioner's attention to what is ready to emerge. In a sense, the client's response is a forward reference that announces the story about to be told. The practitioner listens as intently as possible, knowing that as the story begins, so it will go.

Some examples may illuminate this point. A recent client responded to the opening question by saying, "Are the choices that I am making the ones that I should be making?" Of course, "should" announced the central issue. She was very pleased with what she was doing, yet her mother and aunt insisted that she "should" be doing another thing. At the end of consultation, she had confirmed her commitment to authoring her own life story rather than enacting a plot imposed by powerful others. Another client responded, "Am I doing the right job for now?" The "now" signaled an important meaning. It turned out that he was a person who liked to change his position about every 5 years, joking that he imitated Russia's practice of 5-year plans. He was happy with what he was doing now, yet he was beginning to look ahead to the next move because he did not want to do anything for more than 5 years. At the end of consultation, he expressed his satisfaction with his current position while at the same time he was beginning to envision changing direction in about 2 years.

Still another client responded, "Am I doing something to short-circuit my potential for developing a successful business?" Of course he was, and he knew what had to be done about it. Finally, another client responded, "Am I wasting my time in this graduate program?" She was halfway through a degree program in social work and knew she wanted to go to law school. In the end, she said that she never seriously thought of quitting the graduate program. The consultation helped her articulate that her purpose in life was to be an advocate for those whom society silences. She came to the opinion that she was not wasting her time; rather, she was learning a skill set that would serve her well in her eventual career as a civil rights advocate.

Setting Goals

According to Abraham Lincoln, "A goal properly set is halfway achieved" (quoted in Ziglar, 1997, p. 37). Thus, practitioners should not begin a career story interview until they understand what a client wishes to accomplish through the consultation. Working with each client to explicitly state a mutually agreed upon goal is important for several reasons. First, practitioners must assess whether together they can reach that goal. If it is not something the practitioner can do, then there must be a negotiation or a referral. For example, if a client states that she wants help in résumé writing or a job search, then many practitioners would refer her to a placement specialist who provides that career service. Practitioners do not want to learn after conducting a career story interview that they cannot provide the service sought by the client. If the client seeks academic advice, vocational direction, or career counseling, then practitioners can proceed with the interview. They do so by explaining the structure they will use as they collaboratively pursue the goals that the client has just articulated. Practitioners end the induction into counseling by skillfully articulating a problem statement.

This statement must make the client feel welcome and comfortable and lead to a harmonious working alliance—well begun is half done.

Career construction practitioners have a second use for the response to the opening question. At the end of the session or set of sessions, they restate the client's response to the question and then ask the client, "Have we done this?" This final question revisits the client's reason for seeking counseling and ensures that the practitioner has fulfilled the initial contract. The client should leave the relationship believing that counseling has been successful and satisfactory. Of course, there are many other indicators of effectiveness, particularly action and behavior change outside the consulting room. Yet practitioners should not forget the first one, namely, client satisfaction with what has occurred.

Engaging Emotions

As practitioners work with clients to establish counseling goals, they are also establishing a working alliance by eliciting emotions and offering comfort. They usually try to help clients elaborate their statement of a career problem in feeling terms. Career construction practitioners follow the emotions, those feelings that signal to clients that something requires their attention and move them to seek counseling. Practitioners should attend to the feelings that express the fragmentation of meaning caused by a developmental task, occupational transition, or work trauma. Emotions propel effective counseling and direct practitioners where to go next. So practitioners follow emotions because they show the client's growing edge. Raising awareness of these feelings clarifies the problem a client needs to resolve.

In providing understanding, acceptance, and support for a client's emotional turmoil, practitioners establish a working alliance with which to proceed. Emotions provide the fulcrum for revising the self during counseling. Before meaning may be reorganized and action engaged, feelings must change. Throughout each session, practitioners attend to feelings as a means of perturbing the meaning system to reorganize through new integrations of reason and emotion. To initiate this meaning-making process, practitioners offer comfort while establishing a working alliance.

Comforting is a form of social support that provides emotional relief if needed by the client at the beginning of counseling. Comforting means encouraging the client, normalizing the problem, and reformulating a metaphor (Miceli, Mancini, & Menna, 2009). Practitioners offer comfort by expressing confidence in clients' coping potential and reassurance about their ability to resolve the problem. Practitioners normalize the problem by explaining how it is understandable and maybe even expected. Usually, practitioners help clients view the problem as transitory. In doing so, practitioners do not minimize the problem, just communicate that it is both manageable and temporary. If appropriate, practitioners also explain that the problem is not the client's fault but the result of some life circumstances or a new life stage. Nevertheless, despite the problem's not being a client's fault, the client must have the ability to respond. This responsibility is especially important if the client shows a problem about the problem. Comforting may also include reducing the size of the problem by reformulating a client metaphor or problem statement with a less dramatic term or phrase. Having engaged emotions, set goals, and offered comfort, practitioners are prepared to begin a career story interview.

4

The Career Story Interview

The career story interview consists of stimulus questions that have evolved through 3 decades of practice. Using a protracted trial-and-error approach, I consolidated the questions that worked best. The career construction counseling model theorizes these questions and their sequence. So the career story interview exemplifies putting practice into theory, rather than putting theory into practice (Neimeyer, 2004a).

FRAMEWORK

The rationale for each question in the career story interview alerts practitioners to what they should listen for as clients respond. The questions prompt responses that are not isolated stories; rather, the responses relate to each other in a way that systematically positions them in a framework. Thus, practitioners try to place the responses in a frame that holds everything together, similar to placing puzzle pieces into the puzzle frame. To solve a puzzle, players try to recognize a pattern as they organize fragments of it. So too must practitioners accept the challenge not of solving a puzzle but of using inductive logic to identify a pattern in client responses.

Recognizing patterns and describing themes require a practical skepticism based on common sense; remember, everything could be different. Once practitioners apprehend a possible pattern and career theme in a client's occupational plot, they search to confirm or disconfirm the pattern by identifying repeated episodes in the stories narrated by the client. A novel gets its validity from particulars; so too does a client's career theme.

Veteran practitioners use intuition and induction to choose which stories or story fragments to fit into the frame and how to present that pattern to a client. Vocational guidance that uses test scores rests on analytical thinking and deductive logic. In comparison, career counseling that uses stories rests on intuitive thinking and inductive logic. The problems to be resolved in career counseling are at best only partly explicit. In the highly structured context of vocational guidance, the goal is quite explicit. Guidance personnel use information about individual differences and rule-bound processes to seek an objective solution to the matching problem. They administer tests and inventories to quantitatively compare client abilities and interests to reference standards and normative samples. Interaction with clients revolves around test interpretation regarding their traits. Whereas vocational guidance relies on objective measurement and scores to explain client similarity to nomothetic types and normative groups, career construction practitioners rely on subjective assessment and stories to understand client uniqueness. Career counselors apply clinical judgment to appraise clients' life themes and their pursuit of purpose. They emphasize meaning making over match making. Counseling for career construction explores and elaborates this meaning to clarify the choices and enhance the ability to decide. Because counseling occurs in a less-structured context, it synthesizes intuition and reason.

FORMAT

The career story interview consists of five primary elements of inquiry, each chosen as a gateway to stories on a particular topic. A structured format arranges the five stimulus questions in a frame that helps to elucidate a client's life story and identify career themes. The topics flow smoothly and keep clients actively engaged in self-reflection as they describe themselves to the practitioner. The stimulus questions ask about (1) role models, (2) magazines, (3) favorite book, (4) mottos, and (5) early recollections.

Question 1: Role Models

Following the opening question, practitioners begin a career story interview by asking clients whom they admired when they were young. Asking clients directly to verbalize their self-concept rarely works. So practitioners ask clients to articulate their self-concepts through embodying them in characters whom they have admired. Of course, clients do not at first realize that they are conceptualizing their own selves.

To identify a client's role models, practitioners ask, "Whom did you admire when you were about 6 years old?" If clients do not understand, then practitioners may ask them whom they respected, maybe even enough to imitate. With clients who cannot think of anyone, practitioners may suggest that the model need not be a famous person or fictional character. This frequently leads clients to name a relative, neighbor, or teacher. After a client has named one model, practitioners ask for two additional models. When the client has named three models, practitioners examine each model, in turn, beginning by asking the client, "Describe this person to me." It sometimes takes prodding, so practitioners may say to a client, "Just tell me about the person as you viewed her or him back then. What were they like?" As they characterize their models, clients actually narrate their own self-concepts without realizing it. Even clients who display little self-awareness generally find it easy to talk about their self-concepts as embodied in role models. If a client talks only about what the model did, practitioners specifically ask the client to describe the model's characteristics. If a client talks about how the model behaves today, then practitioners ask clients to remember how they viewed the model when they were young and what first drew them to the model. After eliciting each role model and what the client admired about the model, practitioners may ask for each model, "How are you similar to this person, and how are you different from this person?" Practitioners might also ask a client to explain what all three models share in common.

Clients see themselves more clearly by looking at the characteristics that they admire in their models. In reporting their role models, clients recognize the self. They reveal their self to themselves. To reinforce this recognition, practitioners must remember that it is the descriptions of the role model offered by the client that are critically important. Practitioners must closely listen to hear specifically what a client admires about the model. It is these characteristics that the client has incorporated into his or her blueprint for self-construction. It is not *whom* the client admires but *what* the client admires. Practitioners must be especially careful not to use their own conceptions of the models. It is too easy to assume what a client admires about a famous character. Consider an example about Superman. A practitioner might imagine that the client admires the superpowers, strength, and invulnerability of the "Man of Steel." However, the folk singer Richie Havens explained in 2005 during a performance at the Kent Stage that as a youngster he admired Superman because his hero fought for truth and justice.

Many female practitioners admired Wonder Woman when they were younger. Wonder Woman was created by a Harvard psychologist to model a woman who removed from her body the chains of prejudice, prudery, and man's superiority. William Moulton Marston designed Wonder Woman as an independent woman who gained her power through nutrition and exercise (Joyce, 2008). She used strength and love to conquer evil. Mary Hanna (1994), an American politics professor at Whitman College, once stated that she admired Wonder Woman because she "taught us important lessons: That any woman could acquire strength and skills, that a woman could be in love and still retain her own identity, that family and friends were important, especially the friendship of women" (p. 2-E). Despite the carefully crafted persona and portrayal of Wonder Woman, we cannot assume everyone admires these traits in her. An aeronautical engineer once told me that as a boy he admired Wonder Woman. When I asked what in particular he admired, he responded that he wanted her invisible airplane. He achieved his dream as a member of a team who helped design the Stealth Bomber, his version of an invisible airplane.

A common response to the role model question is the client's mother or father. Practitioners ask clients who identify a parent as a role model to describe the parent, yet they do not count the parent as one of the three role models. They want to hear clients talk about someone other than parents to ensure that the role model was a choice. Parents may be chosen as role models, yet it is more useful to think of them as guides.

It is not unusual for a client to name a famous animal as a model. More than a few students majoring in elementary education have said that they admired the dog Lassie from television show because Lassie always helped children. A psychology student who admired Mighty Mouse eventually became a crisis practitioner so that she too could "save the day." A clinical psychologist eventually earned a PhD by writing his dissertation on interventions for anger management. His alcoholic father's temper had frightened the whole family. The psychologist found a solution for himself in admiring Ferdinand the Bull, who preferred to smell the flowers rather than attack toreadors. A medical student who as a girl admired Miss Piggy because she fought for the underdog eventually opened an inner-city clinic for women.

As clients discuss role models, practitioners should think of what the models imply to form follow-up questions. Effective follow-up questions express inferences, not interpretations, so clients find them thought provoking and occasionally humorous. For example, someone who admires Zorro could be asked, "Do you mask your true identity? Do you rely on a helpful companion? Do you seek to right wrongs against your family?" Client answers to follow-up questions increase practitioners' understanding of client self-concepts. To practice listening to individuals describe their models, readers may listen to podcasts of *Great Lives*, a radio show in which guests discuss their models (http://www.bbc.co.uk/podcasts/series/greatlives).

Question 2: Magazines

Having already considered in the first question the influences and identifications that have shaped a client's self-concept, the second topic in the career story interview addresses vocational interests. From the perspective of career construction theory, interests symbolize a psychosocial variable. In Latin, *inter* means "between," and *est* means "it is." Thus, *interest* means "it is between." In career construction theory (Savickas, in press), interest denotes a psychosocial tensional state between an individual's needs and social opportunities to attain goals that satisfy those needs. Career construction practitioners assess interests by concentrating on the client's preferred environments, namely, those occupational settings in which they believe they may pursue their purpose and fulfill their values. Accordingly, after having learned about a client's self-concept from inquiring about role models, practitioners attend to the types of work settings that capture the client's attention or occupational environments that attract him or her.

There are four ways to appraise vocational interests (Super, 1949). The least effective way is to inventory individuals' preferences for a variety of activities and occupations. Interest inventories assume that respondents have some knowledge of the items and that their self-report will be objective. More effective, yet now rarely used, are interest tests, in which people display greater knowledge about activities that interest them. Better than these two measurements is an assessment of expressed interests, namely, what people say they want to do in the future. The most effective method is to assess manifest interests, that is, inclinations made evident by a person's behavior. When searching a criminal's room, for example, crime investigators look for clues in the residuals left by his or her behaviors. Rather than decor and tidiness, they look to magazines and books to provide the best clues. So in appraising vocational interests, practitioners serve clients better by assessing what clients say and do rather than counting their responses to an inventory or test.

To identify fitting occupational settings, practitioners consider where clients have actually been setting themselves lately. To inquire about preferred occupational settings for a client's possible self, practitioners may ask clients to name favorite magazines, television programs, or websites. Responses to these questions reveal manifest interests, something quite trustworthy in predicting the future. Career construction practitioners usually begin to assess manifest interests by asking clients about their favorite magazines. If a client responds with several publications, then the practitioner typically finds this sufficient. However, if a client rarely reads magazines, the practitioner inquires about television programs. If this fails to elicit meaningful information about preferred settings, then the final option is to ask about frequently visited Web sites. A client's favorite magazines, television programs, or websites are vicarious environments that reveal where clients like to place themselves.

Let us consider magazines first. Magazines vicariously immerse readers in a preferred setting or comfortable environment. People read a magazine to inhabit the world between its covers. In naming favorite magazines, clients tell practitioners about the types of environments that they prefer to inhabit. It is better to try to elicit two or three favorite magazines that a client reads regularly or finds interesting and then ask clients to describe, in turn, what they enjoy reading in each publication. It is important to learn specifically what attracts clients to each magazine. The attraction may be fairly evident when a client names a small-circulation periodical that prints in-depth information about a narrowly defined topic. Examples of specific-interest magazines include *Road and Track, Science, Photography, Psychology Today, Money,* and *Scrapbooks.* When clients name a general-interest magazine that prints diverse information appealing to a broad audience, practitioners must gather more details about the sections that clients enjoy most or read first. For example, if a client names *Time* or *Newsweek* as a favorite magazine, then practitioners should ask the client which section they read first—politics, entertainment, science, medicine, and so on.

Clients who infrequently read magazines usually regularly watch a few television programs. Favorite television shows, similar to favorite magazines, provide information about preferred settings. As a window on the world, television takes viewers places. The programs are called "shows" because they let viewers see different places and observe people addressing specific problems with particular procedures. Watching *This Old House* takes viewers to a physical environment where people engage in strenuous activities to make or repair things. *Divine Designs* shows viewers how an interior designer creates beautiful and stylish rooms. *Crime Scene Investigation* takes viewers to traumatic environments where people use analytical skills to solve mysteries. *Friends* takes viewers to social environments where people use conversational skills to build relationships. *Boston Legal* takes viewers to law offices and political settings where people use persuasive skills to advocate for clients. And finally, *Martha Stewart* takes people to a conventional setting where people use recipes for living and organizing skills to contribute to others. Note that some celebrities, such as Oprah Winfrey (social setting) and Martha Stewart (conventional setting), provide people opportunities to enter a setting through both a television program and a magazine.

Some clients spend more time on a computer than they do reading magazines or watching television. With these clients, practitioners ask where they go on the World Wide Web. In opening a web page, individuals enter a preferred setting. Opening the Internet browser on a client's computer to "pages visited" reveals the manifest interests of the client because it lists the settings entered repeatedly. Individuals keep clicking on what interests them. Practitioners may ask clients to open their web browser, click "control H," click on "Favorites," and copy the list of sites to show the practitioner. After I wrote the previous sentence, I paused to look at my own list of favorite sites. The first was a dictionary and thesaurus site, which I use frequently while writing. Seeing this site, a practitioner could guess that I am interested in words and maybe writing. Of course, the practitioner would be correct, because while writing I am always looking for what the French call the *mot juste*—exactly the right word. The second most visited site was "Shoutcast," an Internet radio site on which I am usually listening to classical or jazz music. The third site was "Travelocity," which I use to make arrangements for frequent travel. So my manifest interests are writing, music, and traveling. A recent client worked in a bookstore. Her favorite websites were www.facebook.com and www.poetry.org. Of course, her vocational interests could be assessed as social and artistic. Her occupational daydream was to become a teacher of creative writing. As the reader may surmise, examining the list may be better than looking at the result of an interest inventory, and it is cheaper.

While listening to and assessing a client's responses about settings, practitioners keep in mind the client's self-concept and how such a self would fare in the settings being discussed. The link between self-concept and vocational interests is typically strong and obvious. For example, a Native American client stated that her favorite television show was *Star Trek* because the crew went where no one else had gone before. Her role model was Pocahontas because she bridged two worlds. Of course, Pocahontas would be a good crew member on the starship *Enterprise*. The client eventually enacted a script as a liaison who maintained communication between two cultural groups. She, like all of us, needed a fitting script to unite self and setting in a meaningful manner. Selection of a setting will profoundly affect the range of stories that may be played out. Settings generate story possibilities and make some scripts inevitable and other scripts impossible. So attention now turns to scripts the client has in mind.

Question 3: Favorite Story

From the first two questions in the career story interview, practitioners have a good idea about a client's self-concept and preferred work environments. The third question deals with enacting that self in that setting by performing a script. So the third topic addresses life scripts. In a sense, the third question addresses the hyphen in the logical positivist paradigm of person–environment fit—that is, the connection between self and setting. It involves the public working out of personal possibilities.

To learn about a client's life scripts, practitioners ask clients to name their favorite story or stories. Practitioners want to learn which stories clients use to shape their lives. After hearing a story title, they ask clients to tell the story. It is important to hear clients tell the story in their own words, even if the practitioner already knows a version of the story. Practitioners listen for how the script unites the client's self and preferred setting. In telling the story, clients usually talk about their own possible futures. Typically, clients' favorite stories portray clearly a central life problem and how they think they might be able to deal with it. Practitioners listen carefully to learn the constructions and comforts of a client's customary script. For example, a female premedical student frequently reread *Gone With the Wind* because the heroine Scarlett O'Hara fascinated her. At an unexamined level, she was dealing with how to be a physician without relinquishing her femininity. She found that this book addressed the fear that her needs for achievement and intimacy conflicted. Another client read Hemingway's *Old*

Man and the Sea as a parable that addressed his creativity and hypersensitivity. He too had to learn to deal with the sharks that would destroy his art. A third client watched the movie *The Godfather* repeatedly because for her it told the story of a man who brings order to a community by providing a value system and explaining rules for living. She became an author and radio personality who commented on society and its values, not a criminal.

Question 4: Mottos

The fourth topic in the career story interview addresses clients' advice to themselves. Practitioners ask clients to state their favorite saying. If clients do not have a motto, practitioners may ask them to repeat a saying they remember hearing or even create a saying in the present moment. With encouragement, even reluctant clients articulate something. The something that they compose in the moment will draw out their own intuitive understanding of how to move forward. Their motto will usually succinctly state their intuitive strategy for beginning to move to the next episode in their occupational plot. The client who admired Pocahontas endorsed the motto "Nothing ventured, nothing gained."

Question 5: Early Recollections

The most personal question is saved for last. After discussing the first four topics, clients have learned to trust their practitioners, and therefore they feel safe enough to reveal more fundamental stories, if not their most fundamental secrets. Also, the sequence of topics in the career story interview builds a momentum that ushers clients into their private preoccupations. Practitioners seek to learn clients' convictions about life by considering nuclear scenes in which clients encapsulate their life stories. These scenes, in the form of early recollections, present to the practitioner a client's perspective on life. Practitioners may view early recollections as metaphors and parables that hold a person's central preoccupation.

Career construction practitioners typically ask for early recollections by stating that they are interested in the client's earliest memories—sort of where the story of their life began. They typically ask for three early recollections because clients often explore their preoccupations and problems in several stories. For each recollection, practitioners have clients describe the setting, action, and results. Practitioners may ask clients to name feelings that they experienced when the action occurred. This often results in clients reporting a feeling that they experience frequently or even the emotion that dominates their lives. Having heard the three early recollections narrated by a client, they then ask the client to review each story and give it a headline that captures its essence. They may ask the client to pretend that the story will appear in tomorrow's newspaper and the editor needs to attach a headline. They also may direct the client to include a verb in the headline. A headline gets its energy from a verb, as a life gets its energy from movement. If the client draws a blank, then the practitioner offers a few suggestions and works with the client to revise it until the client authorizes a headline. Client and practitioner then proceed to compose headlines for the two remaining early recollections.

When practitioners finish headlines for the early recollections, the career story interview is completed. Then practitioners should ask clients if they wish to add anything else. At this point, practitioners should briefly summarize what has been accomplished during the session, orient clients to what will occur during the next session, and assign any homework that might benefit the client in preparing for the next session. It is always necessary and imperative to remind clients that what they have discussed will be held in strict confidence. To prepare for the next session, counselors assess the meaning of the client responses to the career story interview, the topic of Chapter 5.

5

Career Story Assessment

After completing a career story interview and before beginning counseling with clients, practitioners must understand the meaning presented in clients' stories, relate this meaning to the initial reason they sought counseling, and prepare to retell clients' stories in a manner that draws a sharp character sketch, highlights the career theme, and envisions scenarios that extend the occupational plot. Experienced practitioners may make these preparations as they conduct a career story interview so that immediately after finishing the interview they may begin counseling. For example, if they can meet with a client only once, they will spend half the time conducting the interview and half the time counseling with the client. If more than one session is possible, then the tasks of interviewing and counseling may be divided. Typically, career construction practitioners spend the first session eliciting clients' career constructions with the career story interview, the second session narrating to the client a reconstructed story and beginning to coconstruct with the clients an authorized identity narrative, and the third and final session completing counseling and terminating the consultation. They try to have a week between the first and second sessions and 2 to 4 weeks between the second and third sessions. During the week between the first and second sessions, practitioners prepare for the second session by performing an assessment routine that reconstructs client responses to the career story interview into a life portrait that addresses the initial request for counseling.

ASSESSMENT GOALS

To reconstruct a client's responses into a meaningful pattern requires that practitioners assemble the small stories into a large story about the client's occupational plot and career theme. I call this larger story or macronarrative a *life portrait*. Practitioners as narrative artists paint a psychological portrait that brings together seemingly disparate small stories with little apparent connection into a clear and coherent identity narrative. Together, client and practitioner then use the portrait for contemplation and reflection relative to the presenting problem. Usually, studying the life portrait prompts a process of transformative learning with which the client may address the disorienting dilemma or occupational dislocation.

The practitioner composes an initial draft of a life portrait by combining the micronarratives of self, setting, script, and strategy into a higher level macronarrative that incorporates all the small stories. Think of the last time you viewed a special exhibit at an art museum and how the materials were presented. While writing this book I visited an exhibit of Ansel Adams's photographs. The exhibit curator did not merely harvest and display images; he had arranged the materials to reveal an underlying aesthetic. He used narrative competence to transform scattered images and emotions into experiential vignettes that reflected a clear and coherent theme that others could begin to understand.

So too must practitioners arrange clients' small stories in a way that enhances a sense of vitality, reveals meaning, and portrays a life that matters. Absorbing elements from the myriad small stories, practitioners reconstruct a grand story or a narrative identity that provides a resource for living. The reconfiguration—fitting the frame of self, setting, script, and strategy—composes the micronarratives into a macronarrative account that addresses the concerns the client brought to consultation. The micronarratives are reframed to foster understanding, intention, and action. The idea is to let the client's life speak, and specifically speak to the issue at hand. The Ansel Adams photography exhibit included a pertinent story. In 1933, Adams had taken his work to New York City to obtain a critique from the famous modernist photographer Alfred Stieglitz. Adams reported that Stieglitz did not teach him. When Adams showed him his photographs, Stieglitz discussed them and "revealed me to myself." Later in a letter to Stieglitz, Adams (1936) wrote, "My visit with you provoked a sort of revolution in my point of view—perhaps the word simplification would be better. . . . My own work has suddenly become something new to me—new, and exciting as never before." Practitioners share that goal, to organize and portray client stories in a way that reveals clients to themselves.

Finding and articulating the theme in a career requires that practitioners cultivate their narrative competence. An example of this narrative competence comes from the film director Martin Scorsese. He explained narrative competence as transforming scattered images into a clear and coherent story. In making the movie *No Direction Home: Bob Dylan*, Scorsese (2005) had to find the theme in 10 hours of interviews and 300 hours of concert videotapes. To shape the story, Scorsese said that he had "to find the narrative in the footage, in his life" and then tell the story of the artist's journey in a way that speaks to the audience. To do this, he attended closely to the words that Dylan chose to describe his feelings. In the end, Scorsese expressed the core theme with a sentence Dylan spoke in an interview: "I have just been trying to get home." He elaborated this theme using lyrics from Dylan's most famous song, "Like a Rolling Stone," in which the singer uses that metaphor to explain how it feels to be "on your own." Thus, the title of the movie symbolizes Dylan's lifelong struggle to find a "direction home."

To develop the narrative competence displayed by Scorsese (2005) requires that practitioners cultivate three skills. The first skill, *entering the story*, involves the intuition and empathy needed to embrace a story, focus on negative situations and sensations, feel the story's mood, hold its pain, and tolerate ambiguity. The second skill, *understanding the story*, involves recognizing the career theme and using client metaphors to express it. An example of such a metaphor is Dylan's "no direction home." A client who hid from the world behind perfectionism used the metaphor of "putting on a false face." Another client who also hid from the world was a chemistry professor who said, "I took shelter in the university." The third skill, *elaborating meaning,* involves taking multiple perspectives to imagine different interpretations and new meanings that open fresh possibilities for action. In one example of this skill, Pearl Jam's lead singer, Eddie Vedder (2008), explained how audiences' interpretation of his lyrics to the song *Alive* transformed for him the meaning of the words from a curse to a celebration. Similar to Pearl Jam fans, practitioners must serve as an attentive audience for client stories because good listeners improve a story.

Using narrative competence, practitioners portray the client's life and career emphasizing a theme that runs through it. The macronarrative should include a plausible character arc that reconstructs the development of the current situation. A narrative with a sweeping arc presents an overall direction and purpose in life with some sense of movement toward wholeness. Story by story, practitioners reconstruct a large narrative by using slivers of insight punctuated by occasional particulars. The narrative achieves its validity through these particulars. It also should invoke meaning by assimilating experiences and reframing causality to accommodate new understandings. The life portrait should be organized in a way that enhances biographical agency for dealing with the current dilemma. Life portraits should encourage change by opening fresh possibilities for action and even, occasionally, bending the character arc in a hopeful direction. Practitioners must remember that agency resides in the organization of the story. Through clarifying what is at stake and increasing agency, the identity narrative should help clients to gain the courage they need to make life-enhancing decisions and the confidence required to reenter the world.

ASSESSING PATTERNS AND PROBLEMS

Macronarratives incorporate the micronarratives of everyday life into a story that "consolidates our self-understandings, establishes our characteristic range of emotions and goals, and guides our performance on the stage of the social world" (Neimeyer, 2004b, p. 54). Career construction theory (Savickas, 2005) offers a conceptual framework for reconstructing client micronarratives into a comprehensible and coherent identity narrative that helps clients make sense of the past, define the current situation, and envision what to do next. The framework is predicated on three general principles. First, the narrative assimilates the client's current experience. The narrative must coincide sufficiently with a client's current views so that it can be heard. If it varies too far from the preexisting story, the client may not comprehend it and therefore may be unable to use it. Second, the narrative must provide some new material that coherently fills a gap in the story that the client brought for consultation. The new material must elaborate the preexisting story in a way that the client finds credible. The elaborations may bring forward new meanings with which clients can reshape the self and situation. And third, the macronarrative with its new perspective and deeper meaning should invigorate the client to engage in action.

Find Patterns

With client responses to the career story interview in hand, practitioners need to examine the collage of stories to identify a pattern that highlights the core theme in the narrative identity. Although clients' stories usually vary in characters, settings, and circumstances, the stories typically share a theme that each story amplifies. This amplification makes it possible for practitioners to hear a melody embedded in the crackle of stories. Career construction practitioners follow a systematic course of action to fit diverse micronarratives into a macronarrative. They apply a writing routine that guides them in connecting the client's experiences, expectations, and explanations. However, composing a life portrait involves more than just following the steps in this routine. Practitioners must use their own intuition and ideas to organize and animate the elements.

The essential demand in configuring a life portrait is to identify the pattern or career theme that structures the macronarrative. *Pattern* is the latent structure that holds together things that matter most to the client. To compose a meaningful macronarrative for a client's contemplation, practitioners must be able to recognize patterns. Reality presents raw experience that is chaotic, unpredictable, and random. Experience resembles water in flowing without much form. Similar to a glass that contains water, stories contain experience as they shape the stream of consciousness.

Career construction practitioners themselves need a container to hold the client's microstories in some pattern. Imposing a pattern enables practitioners to select events and shape them into a macronarrative. Counseling succeeds when the macronarrative gives clients new ways of looking at their own ideas, not necessarily by providing new ideas. As Proust (1923) stated so well, "The real voyage of discovery consists not in seeking new lands, but in seeing with new eyes" (p. 762). Rogers (1942) explained that practitioners help clients to "look at old facts in new ways" (p. 77), discover new connections between familiar stories, and accept the implications of the new pattern. Counseling illuminates what is already there. Accordingly, the career story assessment protocol provides a framework for illuminating patterns in clients' stories. The elements in the routine are by now well known to the reader: describe a self, place that self in a setting, add a script for the self to enact, and articulate a strategy for setting the script in motion. This protocol for narrative building provides a reliable structure that focuses light on important issues and leaves irrelevant details in the shadows. It provides a structure for considering the microstories in a way that leads to a comprehensible, coherent, and continuous macronarrative.

Again, a caveat is appropriate here. The assessment protocol is meant to increase practitioners' creativity by giving them a starting point and a "security blanket." Practitioners must not rigidly apply the routine. Instead, they should flexibly follow its agenda, remembering what the client seeks from consultation. Being open to varying the routine allows the macronarrative to develop according to client needs, not practitioner preferences. Rigid application of the protocol leads to a macronarrative that is too simple and even clichéd. Certainly, simplification of experience is a goal in composing a macronarrative. Simplification makes it easier to communicate. Yet this simplification, to avoid being simple, must be balanced by organization that preserves the complexity of the life. Order simplifies complexity yet does not need to make it simple. Organization reconfigures complexity into a recognizable design that highlights central meaning.

To organize small stories into an identity narrative, the career story assessment protocol has eight elements. The first two steps in the assessment protocol, and maybe the most important, are to identify the problem by reviewing client goals for counseling and then recognize the pattern by identifying the preoccupation at the base of the character arc.

Review the Client's Goals

Practitioners begin the assessment by reviewing how the client wants to use the counseling experience. These goals focus the subsequent examination of the microstories and the counseling to follow. The goals provide a filter with which to winnow the stories. For example, in response to the introductory question "How can I be useful to you in constructing your career?" one client said that she did not know why she could not choose a major and that she would like help in making a choice. This gave me two points of reference. She wanted me to help her understand why she could not choose as well as to increase her decision-making competence. She seemed immobilized by decisional anxiety. So in reviewing her career stories, I listened to her attitudes toward and experiences with decision making. I was particularly interested in how decision making related to her life themes, one of which was struggling to become free from domination by her mother's goals for her daughter's life. Note that she was not asking, at least initially, for help in identifying a choice. First, she wanted to know what was holding her back. A different client stated that she wanted to identify her strengths and weaknesses because she was having difficulty concentrating on just one part of her job. In short order, her inability to focus on one thing became the central topic as she realized her strength was being a generalist, not a specialist. A third client said that he wanted reassurance that he had selected the right graduate program. Of course, it quickly became apparent that he was already very sure of his choice, yet as a hyperresponsible oldest child, he wanted an authority figure to reassure him about that choice.

Identify Preoccupations

In the second step of the assessment protocol, practitioners consider the client's early recollections to identify preoccupations at the base of the character arc. Adler (1931) wrote that whenever clients requested vocational guidance, he would ask about their memories from the first years of life. He believed that memories of this period show conclusively what they had trained themselves for most continuously. William James believed that from clients' original experience of the world, some feature impressed them so much that from that point forward they used it as an analogy to understand important situations (Barzun, 1983). To improve their lives or change their habits, individuals need to become aware of the analogy for life as a whole and then choose a more effective life orientation (Barzun, 1983, p. 9). Agreeing with both Adler and James, career construction practitioners use early stories to help clients comprehend and evaluate their analogies for life.

Practitioners ask for early recollections because these memories yield stories from when clients were first awakening to life and making up their minds about how their world operates. During this time children figure out the world, from their perspective, and begin to form a persona or mask with which to engage that world. Early recollections portray root experiences that represent the client's basic understandings of themselves, other people, and the world. These touchstone memories serve as prototypes that hold a principle of living and show an example of it in action. Early recollections carry forward into life the lessons learned during childhood. Practitioners want to understand the central meaning that clients keep alive by frequently repeating these analogies to self, each time freshly implanting the meaning in new situations.

Because early recollections portray such fundamental information, practitioners use them as a narrative catalyst to begin the macronarrative. In a sense, practitioners start at the beginning of a client's life story. Well, it is not literally the beginning of the life story that practitioners seek; rather, it is the basic orientation to life. So in examining the early recollections, practitioners concentrate on concerns that constitute the person. These concerns matter so much that they represent the central force in a client's life. They are the preoccupations that define self and identity. In her autobiography, the novelist Agatha Christie (1977) wrote, "I think, myself, that one's memories represent those moments which, insignificant as they may seem, nevertheless represent the inner self as most really oneself" (p. viii).

Early recollections reveal the experiences that have cast a spell on a client's life. These stories with their potent characters are as old as they are deep. The memories awaken often to tell their secrets and to highlight the challenges a client faces. As condensed versions of the life story, they show a life's *leitmotif*—that is, dominant recurring themes. They concentrate attention on the issues that clients cannot ignore. Clients may want help in going around these issues, yet practitioners must help them to address and resolve the issues. The practitioner's job is to bring the memories fully to life so that clients may hear their lessons and deconstruct their imperatives. In the case of career construction counseling, attention turns to how the client may use work to solve the challenge. Drawing on the early recollections, practitioners call forth the mystical essence of a person to infuse meaning and passion into the issues of vocational choice and work adjustment that the client has brought to counseling. The goal is to show clients how to implant their spirit into the mundane activities of daily living.

Why Early Recollections?

Some people ask why career construction practitioners prefer early recollections as opposed to other biographical stories, such as defining moments (McAdams, 1993), nuclear scenes (Carlson, 1981), or success stories (Haldane, 1975). Each of these types of narrative leads to an understanding of the client's preoccupations. However, I prefer early recollections because, unlike stories from even a few years later in life, these foundational stories cut straight to the beating heart of a client's personal drama. They present the central story in a person's oeuvre of self-explanation. As exemplars of a client's prototypical schemata, early recollections report a single, simple, and consistent action without extraneous or distracting details. They are succinct narratives that portray truths by which an individual lives. Similar to parables, early recollections use a concrete narrative to present abstract conclusions about life. In a sense, they contain the client's prescriptions for living, including their beliefs and aspirations. Moreover, early recollections as life parables often possess parallel and symbolic meanings that are unspoken and implicit. Thus, this metaphorical and symbolic language may be used by practitioners to more easily discuss difficult and complex issues.

Because early recollections typically deal with issues that the client experiences as troubling, they often evoke performances of the self. Practitioners learn to expect and even welcome these emotions, assured that as clients narrate early recollections they perform those feelings that they want to deal with at the present moment. Practitioners do well to follow these felt meanings because they show the client's growing edge and signal what needs attention. These emotions are usually the very same ones engaged by the career issue that they brought to consultation. Dealing with these feelings provides a fulcrum for client self-reorganization and energy for novel actions. Inexperienced practitioners are amazed at how often a client's early recollections and accompanying feelings speak directly to the situation being considered. Veteran practitioners know that remembering is an adaptive behavior that enables an individual to deal with the present and prepare for the future. It is for their own self-healing and personal development that clients select stories to tell. From all their available stories, clients narrate those stories that they themselves need to hear. As the presence of the past, early recollections deal with where clients are at now, not where they came from. They also deal with where the person is heading in the future. Many theorists assert that memory of the past relates strongly to projection into the future, with a few theorists even arguing that "memory is first and foremost about the future" (Fivush, 2011, p. 73).

Memories are of the present, not unearthed sources of the present self. Although current activities constantly change memories, the memories themselves always preserve current meaning. Consider an illustration proffered by the finite rule paradox. Wittgenstein (1953) explained that any finite sequence of numbers can be continued in a variety of ways. For example, the number series "2, 4, 8" may be continued legitimately with the numbers 10, 16, or 31. The fourth number changes the meaning of the series that precedes it. So too in life, new experiences may change the meaning of prior ones. People actually reconfigure their memories and their meanings to tell stories about self and society that support current goals and inspire future action. Thus, memories are re-membered or reconstructed to meet the needs of current situations. What comes later reconfigures the meaning of what came before. In telling their recollections, clients read the self backward into the account of a remembered experience. Present telling provides an interpretation from today's perspective. In the act of re-membering, clients actively use past knowledge to make sense of a present situation.

Narrative Truth

An old Jewish adage asks, "What is truer than truth?" The answer is, "the story." Early memories deal with personal truths, which may be told in terms of fictions. Early recollections may not report historical facts; re-membering in the present may actually distort or invent "facts." Instead of facts, early recollections deliver the truth of the past in the present. Career construction practitioners do not mistake these narrative truths for historical facts. For example, one client reported a memory from 5 years of age that involved him lying in his baby crib as he wished for cowboy boots for Christmas. He twisted the facts to symbolize his personal truth of feeling dependent and helpless. Clients do not twist historical facts randomly; instead, they reconstruct the past so that prior events support current choices and lay the groundwork for future moves. Each telling of a narrative has a different context, purpose, and audience. Thus, each telling presents a narrative truth that may fictionalize the past to preserve continuity and coherence in the face of a transition.

Although historical facts need to be accurate, personal truths need only be adequate. It is critical that neither the practitioner nor the client view early recollections as determining the future. Instead, they should view storying as an active attempt at making meaning and shaping the future. The stories guide adaptation by evaluating opportunities and constraints. In telling their stories, clients re-member the past in a way that constructs a possible future. Re-membering is an adaptive behavior that enables individuals to deal with the present and prepare for the future.

Stories Describe Gaps

There are many ways to understand early recollections. Career construction practitioners treat them as X-rays that reveal a hole in a client's heart. The hole, flaw, or mark indicates what the person misses, wants, or lacks.

The early recollections are narratives that arise from a client's desire to heal a wounded heart. Many commentators have explained that stories are about a gap or something that is unexpected. If everything goes as it should, then there is no need for a story. It is when a deviation occurs that a story is needed to make sense of the experience. Career construction practitioners view early recollections as reports of a deviation in the life. These reports often attempt to close the gap between experience and explanation. They explain something that should not have happened yet did.

In most instances, the situation in an early recollection is a problem, actually the problem that the person wishes to solve above all others. However, some people report early recollections that may not properly be called problems, and they flinch at the word *problem*. Nevertheless, within their earliest recollection lies a preoccupation. The more painful the gap in a life, the stronger the person's preoccupation with filling the gap, righting the wrong, or straightening the deviation. People's lives, in many ways, may be viewed as repeated attempts to become more whole as they fill the hole in their hearts, each time repeating a version of the deviation at a higher level of mastery.

So in making sense of a client's early recollections, practitioners seek to understand the conception of life that it nourishes. They do so by viewing the narrative as representing repetition of some thematic issue relative to the current vocational task, occupational transition, or work trauma. It is directly tied to the reason for seeking counseling, and therefore it will be a story that the client needs to hear right now. It is useful to consider the first early recollection from two perspectives. Initially, it may be examined as a possible précis of the current problem. In other words, practitioners ask themselves whether it concisely summarizes the client's present problem. Then the recollection may be reexamined to consider whether it also may be the principal preoccupation that forms the base of the character arc. Usually, it is easy to recognize both the perennial preoccupation and present problem in the single recollection. Sometimes only one or the other seems evident. There is always something important embedded in the recollection.

Using the early recollection as a narrative catalyst, practitioners may amplify what is remarkable in the story to increase realization and reevaluation. In applying the Jungian technique of amplification, practitioners gather all the knowledge they can about a particular verbal element or image. They concentrate on the first verb and ask, "Where have I heard this before?" I recently finished working with a client who started his first early recollection by saying, "I remember moving to a new house." I amplified the verb *moving*, thinking that it represented a frequent action in his life. So for this client, I concentrated on him being sensitive to moving, enjoying movement, liking to be on the move, being a mover and shaker, being moved, having motivation, and hating being immobile. I also realized that the move he described was to a new house. So moving to new situations is an important theme, probably with both positive and negative elements. In the second early recollection, he recalled his difficulty in adjusting to the move. One day he was riding his bike up the driveway, peddling as fast as he could to avoid being sucked downhill into a morass of trouble. These two recollections re-presented his career problem of having just moved to yet another new job and working as hard as he could yet being pulled down by forces beyond his control.

A second example comes from a student who had just completed a semester-long course on career construction counseling. As he was leaving the final examination, he told me that he did not put much stock in using early recollections. I asked him to tell me his earliest recollection. He replied, "Someone was changing my diaper and I did not want it changed. Make something out of that!" Hearing him repeat twice the verb *change*, I amplified it. I said that change, displacement, development, transformation, and transition preoccupied him, especially those instances in which he and other people did not want to change. He immediately said that his major interest in psychology was transitions, and that he planned to conduct his dissertation research on refugees who were forced to leave their homes and move to the United States. He left the classroom thinking about changing his mind regarding the usefulness of early recollections.

Story Sequence Analysis

It is a good practice to ask clients for three early recollections because people often explore their preoccupations in several stories. The first early recollection announces the issue that concerns the client more than any other issue—that is, the preoccupation. The second recollection often, but not always, repeats that concern or elaborates it with a second story. The third recollection frequently presents a potential solution. As an example, recall the client who in his first recollection moved to a new house and in his second recollection had trouble establishing himself there. His third recollection pointed to a potential solution. In that recollection, he told how his mother bought him several birthday cards when he was four. When she read them to him, he was amazed that you could put speech on paper and understand it. He said, "I think that this filled me with a sense of wonder." Maybe words on paper can solve the problem of being pulled down. Having spent his career moving in and out of more than 10 positions in the same occupation, at age 55 he sought consultation about an occupational change. He was financially secure and wanted to pursue something new. In short order, it became clear that the something new was becoming a motivational speaker and author. His specialty would be how to adjust to new situations without falling down. Whether or not this sequence of presentation holds for a particular client, practitioners should look for a problem statement in the first recollection, its repetition in the second recollection, and its resolution in the third recollection. Deeper meaning may be found in sequences that show a strand that holds the three recollections together.

Many career construction practitioners find it particularly helpful to read in order the three headlines that clients have given to their earliest recollections. Because the headlines distill the story, reading them in sequence often tells a larger story. Consider the example of a research scientist who sought consultation because she was considering changing careers. She did not enjoy her work or colleagues and was unsuccessful in securing research funds from granting agencies. The headlines to her three early recollections in order read "The Responsible One," "She Did Not Know How to Do It," and "Feeling Stupid." Reading these sentences back to her proved to be a powerful narrative catalyst. She concluded that her employer held her responsible for doing something she could not do, which left her feeling stupid. Following career counseling, she quickly changed occupations from research scientist to professor of science at a small liberal arts college. She enjoyed immediate success as a professor. And even more, she felt satisfaction serving as an academic advisor responsible for helping students match their abilities to different majors. In analyzing a story sequence such as this, practitioners may be guided by the principles and methods discussed by Arnold (1962). Practitioners who would like to improve their skill at using early recollections in general might also consult a book by Clark (2002) concerning their use in counseling and psychotherapy.

A Qualification

I suggest that practitioners routinely inquire about early recollections. Most clients protect themselves by sharing early recollections that relate to the issues at hand and with which they themselves are ready to deal. Then, during the assessment routine, practitioners can decide if they will address the preoccupations with the client and if so, how. According to the client's emotional readiness and the practitioner's comfort, the early recollections may be discussed at varying levels of depth, from the superficial to the profound. Nevertheless, even if the early recollections are not discussed at all during counseling, understanding the client's core concerns is useful in drawing a sensitive life portrait.

Some practitioners disagree with this suggestion, believing that beginning practitioners may not be ready to confront the problems or able to handle the pain that clients reveal in early recollections. The counseling relationship provides a holding environment, one that culturally structures discussion of difficult stories. Practitioners must be able to hold the client story and address it authentically. Early recollections routinely evoke self-interpretations that clients perform as felt meaning. So if a practitioner is not prepared to deal with strong emotions, then that practitioner should not ask about early recollections. If the practitioner takes this option, and sometimes it is necessary because of time limitations, then the practitioner looks for the problem and preoccupation in the responses to the first question about role models. The models present the client's proposed solution to the issue, so practitioners may concentrate just on the resolution and avoid directly addressing the client's preoccupation and pain. For example, if a client models a heroine's courage, it implies that the early recollection might be about feeling scared. Other common examples are extroverted models who resolve shyness issues or independent models who resolve dependency issues.

To substantiate the caveat about using early recollections, consider one told by a client who recalled that one day after returning home from the first grade, she could not find her mother. Searching the whole house, she eventually discovered her mother lying on a bathroom floor with blood flowing from her cut wrists. The child stood helplessly, watching her mother die. The practitioner must be prepared to hold this pain so that the client can consider it as a nuclear scene in her life story. If the practitioner feels overwhelmed by the story, then the practitioner becomes less effective. Of course, a practitioner feeling overwhelmed still can express this shared pain and try to process the emotions with the client. However, this is not the goal of career construction counseling. In counseling with the client who had passively witnessed her mother's last moments of life, the goal was to meet the client's request for help in shaping her career. Using this early recollection, it became clear that she wished to turn passivity to activity by dealing with dying people. I thought that she might be interested in working at suicide prevention, but the client's reaction indicated that suicide prevention did not fully address the pain of watching helplessly as her mother died. She told me a secret that she had never shared with anyone. She aspired to become a "midwife for death." She wanted to be with dying people and, if she could, help them meet death with grace and dignity. She chose hospice work for her career, and in a way she healed herself each time she helped a patient die with dignity. Having assessed a client's problems and preoccupations, the practitioner next considers the solutions the client is currently living.

6

Assessment of Solutions

The third step in the assessment protocol identifies client solutions to the problems posed in their early recollections. With a client's pre-occupations in mind, practitioners begin to consider responses to the question about role model. This question inquires about how clients have built a self that is their own resource for living. As the architects of their own character, individuals select role models who provide blueprints for how to solve problems that they themselves now face. Models are selected because they portray tentative solutions to the client's predicament in life. Clients identify these key figures as ego ideals, imitate some of their salient behaviors, and eventually include their features in their own self-concepts. Clients cannot fully comprehend their emergent self from within, so career construction counseling holds up role models as a metaphorical mirror in which they may observe themselves. How clients describe their role models reveals core elements in their own self-concepts. Looking at their role models helps them to see the best in themselves. The systematic reconstruction of a client's "self" in the life portrait encourages clients to substantiate their self-concepts and high-light their characteristics.

The phrase *role model* has become an expression made trite through overuse. The profound meaning of *role model* signifies a blueprint or original pattern that individuals use to design themselves. As explained earlier, a self is a project, not a given. Acting as architects of the self, individuals must select certain blueprints for self-design. They then build that self by adopting and rehearsing the models' characteristics until the characteristics become their own. When the bodybuilder and actor Steve Reeves died in 2000, California governor Arnold Schwarzenegger (2001) fondly remembered his role model with the following posting on his website:

> As a teenager, I grew up with Steve Reeves. He was the hero I cheered for in the cinema, and the champion bodybuilder whose pictures hung in my room, inspiring and challenging me to be the best. His remarkable accomplishments allowed me a sense of what was possible when others around me didn't always understand my dreams. In that sense, Steve Reeves has been part of everything I've ever been fortunate enough to achieve. Steve Reeves was an inspiration to me and will continue to be part of all of our futures. The world has lost more than a man, they have lost a true hero.

To investigate how a person conceptualizes the self, practitioners look to the blueprints and models used by clients early in the process of self-construction. From this perspective, practitioners view role models as the first career choice. Clients were attracted to models who shared their plight yet had found a way to flourish. Heroes and heroines provide a road map to adulthood because they model solutions to clients' own predicaments in growing up. For many people, we can say they have a problem that concerns them more than any other problem. For other people, we are safer saying that they have an issue that preoccupies them. Whichever is the case, in many ways their lives become a solution to that problem or manifestation of that preoccupation. In responding to questions about role models, clients implicitly tell practitioners about the problems that they wish to solve above all else. The characteristics modeled by the heroine or hero constitute the means that a client believes necessary to resolve his or her own predicaments. Thus, it is useful to listen for how these qualities are used in later stories.

ROLE MODELS AND GUIDES

Role models are imaginative resources that individuals use to inform and shape their identities. For example, Bebe Neuwirth, who played Lilith on the television show *Frasier* and starred in the Broadway musical *Chicago*, described her hero Bob Fosse thus:

> I can't quite express just how deeply everything is sort of hinged on what he did, my seeing what he did when I was 13 and going "Okay, that's me up on that stage. I know that. That's who I am." I just found myself. (CBS, 2010)

Similar to Neuwirth, people take meaning from their models to make sense of their own lives. An individual chooses a model from the repertoire of heroines and heroes presented by society. These models possess an almost mythic dimension as they represent national types or predilections that show characteristic methods to pursue goals and solve problems. McAdams (2008) explained how these heroes come to represent goals, as exemplified by Ben Franklin and Horatio Alger, who sought success; Ralph Waldo Emerson and Oprah Winfrey, who sought health; Mother Teresa, who sought salvation; and Martin Luther King, Jr., who sought social justice. The models presented by a society are powerful myths that are easy to generalize so that many different people can imitate the models to address the deep and vexing issues they face in childhood and early adolescence. Individuals actually adopt and adapt these general models to fit the specific meaning that they require and then manifest those characteristics in a form they prefer. As an archetypal pattern, the models sustain meaning with an enduring vitality.

Societies continually update old models and provide new ones. Take, for example, the motion picture *Coraline* (Jennings, Selick, & Gaiman, 2009). In early 2009, British and U.S. societies saw an attempt to add a new heroine to pursue a perennial goal. Coraline became a new model of the gutsy girl. Previous generations learned how Lewis Carroll's Alice went down the rabbit hole and Frank Baum's Dorothy went to Oz. Henry Selick, director of *Coraline*, stated,

> Alice and Dorothy are important characters in my life, and in our common culture. . . . Like Coraline, they want to know what is through the door or around the corner. They are plucky girls who have to get in the middle of it. (quoted in Wloszczyna, 2009, p. D-1)

According to Wloszczyna (2009), Coraline is the perfect heroine for hard times. As intended, there is a lesson in Coraline and her adventure, a lesson that serves tremulous young girls as a potential role model for moving from anxiety to adventure.

Role models teach individuals enduring lessons that they hold close to their hearts. They reveal the original enthusiasms of childhood, those that remain with the client today. Role models inspire and interest young people because they show a way forward. So the choice of role models is indeed a decision about self-construction and the role one prefers to play in life's drama. In his autobiography, the philosopher John Stuart Mill (1873/1990) discussed the importance of having a hero to admire and imitate. He explained that he himself admired Condorcet's (1787) *Life of Turgot:*

> The heroic virtue of these glorious representatives of the opinions with which I sympathized, deeply affected me, and I perpetually recurred to them as others do to a favorite poem, when needing to be carried up into an elevated region of feeling and thought. (Mill, 1873/1990, p. 76)

John Stuart Mill demonstrated how role models may remain a presence in our lives when he told John Morley (1918) "that in his younger days, when he was inclined to fall into low spirits, he turned to Condorcet's *Life of Turgot;* it infallibly restored his possession of himself" (p. 57).

The attraction to a role model leads to imitation in fantasy and play, which through repetition and rehearsal develops skills, abilities, and habits. Centuries ago, Plato (380 BCE/2007) explained "how imitation, beginning in early youth and continuing far into life, at length grows into habits and become a second nature, affecting body, voice, and mind" (p. 78). In musical performers we can even see the emulation of a singing style. As youngsters, both Michael Bublé and Kevin Spacey admired Bobby Darin. Bublé's singing style and repertoire resemble

Darin's, and Spacey did his own singing in the movie about Darin, *Beyond the Sea* (Spacey, 2004).

Guides Versus Models

Clients may identify a parent as a role model, yet it is easier to think of the parent as a guide (Powers, Griffith, & Maybell, 1994). Most practitioners hear descriptions of guides as the client's first ideas about what it means to be a man or a woman. Often the family drama lies in these descriptions of social roles. For example, one client described his father as tough and his mother as tender. He loved them both and felt torn between their contradictory styles of relating to other people and situations. He wanted to please his father by being tough, yet he feared that this would displease his mother, who wanted him to be tender. His way of integrating these contradictory poses was to imitate Robin Hood, whom he described as tough in defeating villains yet tender in helping people in need. The client eventually directed a social work agency, a role he enacted in a tough yet tender manner. As a second example, recall the client who admired Pocahontas because she bridged two worlds. That client was the daughter of an Apache mother and Irish father. She started bridging worlds the day that she was born.

Sometimes it may be useful to have a client compare parental guides to role models. Differences between the guide and model reveal the link between that client's problems and goals and thus map the client's line of movement from a felt minus to a perceived plus. Fundamentally, career construction practitioners view the role model as the first career choice, unlike a parental guide, who is not a choice but a given in the client's life. The parents or parental figures choose the client, not the other way around.

Parental guides are influences, whereas role models are identifications. Internalization of the world means modeling self on objects in the world. A person constructs a self in an environment of other people, particularly parents. The psychological processes used to internalize parental guides differ from the processes used to internalize role models. The main methods for internalization are introjection and incorporation. Guides are internalized as introjects because they are swallowed whole (Wallis & Poulton, 2001). Thus, the introject becomes, in inner space, a representation of that guide. In a sense, an introject internalizes more than a representation of the guide; it internalizes the individual's relationship with the guide. The individual may actually engage in dialogues with the internalized representation.

In contrast to the influence of introjected guides, role models are incorporated identifications. Although introjects are taken in by the person, they are never accepted as their own choices. In comparison, individuals experience identifications as freely chosen images that reflect aspects of themselves. Incorporation of models is a core process of self-construction. One modifies the self to resemble the model, but the model remains external, unlike a guide, who becomes an inner other. In a sense, children *take in* guides but *take on* some characteristics of models with whom they identify. Guides are representations of people that are stored in the mind as percepts. In comparison, models are incorporated as concepts that alter the person and structure the self. Identification includes changing the self to resemble the other, either consciously or unconsciously. The etymology of identification rests on *idem*, Latin for "the same." Identification, or the process of producing sameness with some model, occurs as the self incorporates, as a rather permanent part of itself, characteristics of the other. Individuals identify with some features of the other and direct their life toward achieving similar things. The intention is to address their own problems, and they identify with and emulate those role models who have solved the same problems in growing up that they themselves now face.

Some guides—that is, parents—consciously try to present role models for their children to emulate. For example, the novelist Brad Meltzer explained that he labored long and hard to choose people he wanted his son to admire. Hoping to inspire his son, he published the results in a book entitled *Heroes for My Son* (Meltzer, 2010). Of course, he included his own heroes, such as Jerry Seigel and Joe Shuster, who invented *Superman.* Meltzer wrote that these two teenagers were not affluent, good looking, or popular, yet as two best friends with one dream, they gave the world something in which to believe. Comic book readers know Brad

Meltzer from *Identity Crisis,* a five-issue limited series about the Justice League (including Superman; Meltzer, 2005). One must wonder how often a child selects a parent's role model as his or her own.

Amalgamating Models and Guides

When inquiring about role models, it is best to elicit three models because a client's self and self-concept are a complex amalgam of influences and identifications. An example may be helpful here. As Seigel and Shuster were designing the character whom they would eventually name Superman, they looked for characteristics to incorporate into their superhero. In the end, they designed Superman as a combination of Tarzan's hair, Flash Gordon's outfit, and a weightlifter's black boots (Nobleman, 2008). When considering the responses in which a client describes three role models, practitioners ponder how the client has integrated these characteristics or fragments of a character into a cohesive and unitary self. The separate adjectives that clients use to describe their role models represent self-selected characteristics. Role playing, or imitating the model, mobilizes interests and activities that lead to skill development and confidence to address problems in growing up. During adolescence and emerging adulthood, individuals unify their collection of selective identifications into a coherent whole. This is not a summing up but a synthesis, a configuration that reconciles multiple abstractions to produce an integrative solution to the problems in growing up.

Two examples of self-construction through amalgamation of identifications appeared during the months in which I was writing this chapter. As you read the stories about *60 Minutes* producer Don Hewitt and Supreme Court Justice Sonia Sotomayor, note that each one chose both a male and a female role model. First, consider the models of Don Hewitt. On August 23, 2009, the television program *60 Minutes* (CBS, 2009) honored the memory of its producer, who had died August 19. Hewitt had combined news with show business to create *60 Minutes,* television's first newsmagazine. As a young boy growing up in New York City, Hewitt found his role models in movies. He identified with rascals who had the moxie to beat the system. Hewitt commented, "I never knew whether I wanted to be Julian Marsh, the dictatorial Broadway director who mounted a successful stage production of a musical extravaganza at the height of the Depression, or Hildy Johnson, the reporter in *His Girl Friday*." Impresario Julian Marsh in *42nd Street* was surrounded by bright lights and Broadway showgirls. Hildy Johnson, like Don's father, came from the newspaper world. She thrived in a newsroom with snappy talk and by scooping the competition. In 1948, CBS put on its first televised newscast; Hewitt was 25, with some wartime reporting experience. A friend suggested that he visit the CBS news studio, which he remembered thus: "As I walked in, I couldn't believe it. There were lights and cameras and makeup people and it looked like a Hollywood set. And I fell in love," Hewitt remembered. And the best thing was that he no longer had to choose between being ace reporter Hildy Johnson or Broadway star maker Julian Marsh. "I thought, 'Oh my God, in television you can be both of them.' And I got hired," Hewitt later recalled. In creating *60 Minutes* Hewitt made a niche for himself that enabled him to behave as an amalgam of newsman and showman as well as editor and producer.

During her confirmation hearings for a seat on the U.S. Supreme Court, Justice Sonia Sotomayor recalled her childhood identifications. At an early age she had aspired to become a detective, identifying with Nancy Drew in the popular children's mystery series. But at age 8, Sotomayer was diagnosed with diabetes and told that she would not be able to become a detective. Sotomayor recalled that another fictional character inspired her next choice.

> I noticed that Perry Mason was involved in a lot of the same kinds of investigative work that I had been fascinated with reading Nancy Drew, so I decided to become a lawyer. Once I focused on becoming a lawyer, I never deviated from that goal. (CNNPolitics, 2009)

Sotomayor shaped her version of being a lawyer to involve plenty of investigative work rather than just concentrating on enterprising activities. Her older brother Juan observed that she also incorporated Nancy's traits of industriousness and persistence.

Not everyone who identified with Nancy Drew focused on her investigative talents or persistence. Two writers for *Good Morning America*,

Shipman and Rucci (2009), provided several examples. *60 Minutes* host Diane Sawyer admired Nancy Drew for being "clever, gutsy, and decidedly independent." Supreme Court Justice Ruth Bader Ginsberg incorporated from Nancy's modeling the characteristic of being "fearless." At-large editor of *O Magazine* Gayle King focused on "bravery," stating that "I was always impressed with her bravery, because I was not a brave kid . . . and I used to marvel that she could go in the dark with a flashlight to the unknown. I'm still not very brave." Actress Ellen Barkin identified with the fact that "Nancy Drew had a job. She was the first woman I was aware of that had a job, she wasn't paid for it, but she was a woman with a purpose."

In summary, role models reveal the characteristics that clients think necessary to overcome their main problems or chief preoccupations. Individuals imitate and rehearse the model's characteristics because the features directly address their own concerns. This is why fearful people become courageous and shy people become outgoing. There is no need for courage unless there is fear. There is no need to be outgoing unless one feels like staying inside. So career construction counseling enables clients to see themselves more clearly by looking at what they have *taken in* from their parental guides and *taken on* from their role models.

SKETCHING A SELF

Client descriptions of their role models reveal core conceptions of their selves. Practitioners amalgamate these concepts into a verbal sketch that portrays a brief, general account of a client. In sketching the contours of a self, practitioners identify core self-conceptions based on primacy and repetition. They begin by identifying the first thing a client says about the first role model. Primacy usually accompanies importance. Similar to the first verb in the first early recollection, the first adjective in a role model description signals an important characteristic. In addition to primacy, frequency also indicates importance as it emphasizes salient self-conceptions. As practitioners review the set of descriptions for the three role models, they circle repeated words and similar phrases. Then, having a set of self-relevant descriptions based on primacy and frequency, practitioners formulate a brief and sharply drawn characterization of the client's self-concept. In later stories about stage and script, they will listen for how the client uses these qualities.

Two examples may be useful here. The first comes from a physician who sought consultation because she did not enjoy her medical practice. Her first role model was Dr. Sharp, who lived next door to her family as she was growing up. In describing Dr. Sharp, she said that he "kept it going," created community rituals, cared about his neighbors, was active in the community, and had a peaceful family with no conflict. When I said that these characteristics sounded more similar to a social worker than a physician, she agreed and said that was her problem. In due course, she resolved the problem by closing her medical practice and becoming an associate dean of students at a medical school. That position required her MD and made use of her experience as a physician, yet more importantly it manifested her self-concept as she created rituals and traditions for the school, resolved conflicts to maintain the peace, kept good things going, and fostered a sense of community among the students, faculty, and staff.

A second example of role models comes from an African American client who worked as a photographer and wanted to discuss starting his own business. He admired Pablo Picasso and Dizzy Gillespie. The client stated that he had "patterned his life after Dizzy" by being true to himself yet continuing to give to others. He admired Picasso because he changed people's perceptions. The client played one night a week at a local jazz club, where he said he tried to change listeners' perceptions of music. He decided to open a photography studio where he could "give to others" in his own way.

Addressing Secrets

Sometimes as clients remember significant people from their childhood, they wrestle with their past. They may struggle to dislodge habitual misconceptions set solid in childhood by the significant figures who populated their first world. Occasionally during this struggle, clients reveal a story that they have kept to themselves, a secret that makes the life whole. These secrets more often than not involve sexual abuse. Consider an example from an African American social worker who sought consultation about whether to accept a management position. Her roles models were the actress Doris Day, her Aunt Harriet, and her eighth grade teacher Mrs. Evans. The client described Doris Day as a woman who told men where to go, a career woman who lived her own way, and a bouncy individual. Aunt Harriet taught school, was bright, and "what she did, she did well." Mrs. Evans was well educated and had good values and principles. So one may surmise a self-concept of independence, education, enthusiasm, and integrity. She confirmed this conjecture with additional stories and then concluded that as an assertive and independent career woman, she would make a good administrator. In other words, the proposed promotion would implement her self-concept.

Although primacy and repetition routinely point to salient conceptions, occasionally so does omission. This client omitted saying what Aunt Harriet did not do well. She pointed to the omission by stating, "What she did, she did well." I asked the client what Aunt Harriet did not do well. She hesitantly told me that Aunt Harriet's husband had raped her many times while she was in junior high school. Aunt Harriet knew what her husband was doing yet did nothing about it. Aunt Harriet was her role model in every other way. What her aunt did, she did well. It was what her aunt failed to do that propelled her niece on a mission to do for others what she wished Aunt Harriet had done for her. The client explained how her two other models, Doris Day and Mrs. Evans, showed her how to solve her problem. She learned to tell men where to go and developed the integrity and courage to stand up for herself and to fight for other women. As a social worker, she helped abused girls and women. And she believed that as an administrator and advocate, she could have more influence on public policy and professional practice relevant to abused women. She would continue to tell men like Aunt Harriet's husband where to go.

A second example of the question about role models eliciting a secret comes from a Hispanic man who worked as an executive. One of his first role models was a friendly neighbor whom he had greatly admired. Unfortunately, this trusted mentor slipped his hand in the boy's pants as they were walking home from a movie theater. The boy never reported this incident or spoke of it to anyone. It was mentioned during a consultation about why he did not have a passion to pursue. He enjoyed his work yet felt something important was missing. Of course, after telling the story that could not be told, he recognized how he had been smothering a searing pain. Revealing his secret ignited his passion to help abused boys, an undertaking that consumed his free time and shaped important community programs. This volunteer work filled a hole in his heart and even enabled him to more fully enjoy his "day job." These two clients illustrate how secrets from the past may be animated in the present as well as how career construction counseling may help clients rework childhood traumas.

Connecting Problems to Solutions

Clearly, the social worker's role models showed her a way to solve her problems in growing up. For virtually every client, the role models portray solutions to their early problems and continuing preoccupations. Thus, career construction practitioners must be diligent in understanding how clients' role models solve the problems articulated in their early recollections. Practitioners always attempt to connect a client's self-conceptualizations directly to the first early recollection to determine how these characteristics address the preoccupation. It is at this point that practitioners begin to form an idea about the pattern and progress in a client's life. The old is never fully transcended or replaced; it remains in the heart. The psychoanalyst Hans Loewald (1960) once commented that the work of therapy is to turn ghosts into ancestors. This is what practitioners try to do with the preoccupation in the earliest recollections. They recast the story of clients' self-constitutive narrative as a successful response to the concerns revealed in the early recollections. The goal is to help clients understand how they built a self to deal with their problems and preoccupations as well as soothe their anxieties. Practitioners connect the early recollections and role models to portray how the self whom the client constructed became a hero or heroine who can solve the problems stated in the early recollection. The essence of that self is portrayed as being a solution to problems encountered. At the simplest level, one could use the example of a frightening early recollection being linked to brave role models. Bravery solves the fear. In short, the early recollections state the problem that the self reflected from role models proposes to solve. To make this point and allow readers some practice at tracing character arcs, three examples follow.

The first client's character arc moved from helpless to helpful. She reported the following three early recollections:

- I remember falling into my uncle's pool, not knowing how to swim, and falling slowly to the bottom, only to look up and see someone's arm pull me out. I was scared and helpless.
- I remember the frustration of learning to ride a bike, and my father pushing me, and being scared at first and then exalted at the realization that I could ride a bike myself.
- I remember a moment when my father came home from work. I jumped out of bed to meet him at the door and was so happy that he was finally home. I felt safe and protected.

Note that the first two memories brought feelings of being helpless (repeated in two memories), falling to the bottom, and feeling scared. She felt safe and protected at home, yet her father pushed her to ride, after which she felt exalted at her achievement. Her first role model was Dorothy from *The Wizard of Oz* (LeRoy & Fleming, 1939) because "she was independent and able to help others achieve what was lacking in their lives. She had the courage to fight the Wicked Witch and travel to an unknown land." Dorothy modeled independence, not helplessness, as well as courage, not fear. The client could ride to a different place and while there do for others what her father did for her—that is, help them achieve what they lacked in their lives. Her rehearsal prepared her well for her work as a psychotherapist, in which she provides a secure base and encourages clients to ride to a different place. Today, she pulls others out of trouble.

A second client's character arc moved from not believing in others to believing in herself. She reported the following early recollection:

I was in kindergarten, and I remember getting in an argument with my mom as a little kid. We were driving in the car, and she and my aunt decided to tell me that Santa did not exist. Their reason for doing so was that they did not want me to grow up and believe that

Jesus was a Christmas myth like Santa. I remember being sad and angry because I wanted to believe in Santa still. I felt my mom stole that childhood belief away from me, and now I could not fit in. I was not ready to not believe in Santa.

The client admired Cinderella because "she overcame so much. She was genuine and caring. Others did not treat her the way she deserved to be treated, yet she stayed who she was and did not lose sight of her dreams." For the client, Cinderella modeled how to act when others did not treat her as they should and how to deal with not fitting in by being genuine and remaining true to your dreams. Her rehearsal prepared her well for her work as an actress, and despite many rejections she remains true to her dream. Today, she believes in herself.

A third client's character arc moved from conflict to conciliation. She reported the following early recollection:

> I remember my brother running away from home and disobeying my dad. It got so bad that they started fistfighting in the upstairs hallway, and I remember them rolling around the ground fighting. I remember my mom yelling at them to stop. I remember feeling scared that this was happening and seeing how angry both of them were. I felt helpless because I just stood by and watched. I just wanted to stop it.

And stop it she does. The client admired Smurfette because

> she had an upbeat personality even in times of struggle. She helped all the other Smurfs quite a bit with their projects and was nice and friendly to everyone, even if they were not nice to her. And usually she was always right in a situation and had the best perspective and taught the other Smurfs life lessons.

Her second model was the mother from the Muppet babies because she

> always came to the scene to help. She watched over the kids and gave them a different perspective when they were being mischievous. After she left, the Muppet babies would always want to do the right thing because of what she said.

Both Smurfette and Muppet Mom modeled how to deal with anger, conflict, and fear. The client went from watching helplessly to helping others in conflict by using her upbeat personality and teaching life lessons. Her rehearsals as Smurfette and Muppet Mom prepared her well for work as a college residence hall director, where she offers new perspectives to students in trouble. The psychotherapist, actress, and residence hall director each found an occupational setting in which they could be themselves and use their personal solutions on the job. This is the next task in the assessment routine—namely, identifying interesting settings in which the client may place the self in a story.

7

Assessment of Settings, Scripts, and Scenarios

Having articulated a client's self-concept and traced the character arc, practitioners proceed to the fourth element in the assessment protocol. They assess the educational and vocational interests that clients manifest in their favorite magazines, television shows, or websites. Descriptions of these vicarious environments suggest clients' interest in preferred work settings and attractive occupational environments. Remember that *inter est* means "it is between." Interests link personal processes of meaning making to a social ecology that can sustain them. Vocational interests are important because they guide clients' approach behavior. The client's goal is to select and then occupy the most advantageous setting. Settings differ in their requirements, routines, and rewards. The ideal setting accommodates clients' strengths and weaknesses, involves them in engaging routines, and provides motivating rewards. As in a novel, character must be true to setting. It is the same in careers; the self and setting must be harmonious. Holland (1997) called the harmony between self and setting *congruence,* whereas Lofquist and Dawis (1991) called it *correspondence,* meaning that the person and environment are mutually responsive to each other. Super, Starishevsky, Matlin, and Jordaan, (1963) preferred the term *incorporation,* meaning that the setting must substantiate an individual's self-concept. Career construction theory states that occupational settings should provide a secure niche that holds individuals.

Career construction theory likens an occupational setting to a holding environment to emphasize the dynamics and core function of an environment. An occupational setting is not a static backdrop. It is more than a frame around a self-portrait. A setting presents a cultural context that makes some things possible and other things impossible. Setting offers both comforts and constraints as it channels action possibilities. Moreover, a setting calls forth certain kinds of characters and prototypical workers. For example, a classroom calls for a person with interpersonal skills, and an auto shop calls for a person with mechanical skills.

PLACES, PEOPLE, PROBLEMS, AND PROCEDURES

To help clients identify fitting niches, practitioners may analyze the settings that attract their interests along four dimensions: places, people, problems, and procedures. They want to learn from assessing clients' vocational interests the places in which they want to work, the people with whom they wish to interact, the problems they prefer to address, and the procedures they like to use.

People vary in their preferences for places along dimensions such as outdoor versus indoor, clean versus sullied, neat versus cluttered, sedentary versus active, isolated versus gregarious, and safe versus hazardous. For example, an individual who prefers a workplace that is outdoor, clean, neat, sedentary, isolated, and hazardous might explore the occupation of truck driver. Preferences regarding place or workspace are usually quite obvious from clients' answers to questions about magazines, television programs, and websites.

More important and less obvious than physical space are preferences regarding coworkers. As Schneider (1987) explained, "the people make the place." So the most important element of a setting is the people who occupy it. Organizational culture reflects the unique collection of people who gather together. The other people must welcome and comfortably interact with the client. This idea is sometimes expressed using the aphorism "Birds of a feather flock together." In short, occupational settings attract, select, and retain those people who share the values of the incumbents.

An example of how people make a setting interesting and prompt approach behaviors comes from a career counseling session with a college junior who wanted to select a graduate program. When I asked him how he selected his undergraduate major, his reply gave a précis of Schneider's (1987) attraction–selection–attrition theory. The student reported that during his first year, he took five courses each semester. He selected each of the 10 courses from different academic departments. During the two semesters, he kept track of the time he arrived at a class and what time he left it. He had surmised that he should major in the department that offered the course for which he arrived the earliest and left the latest and minor in the department that offered the course where he spent the second most time. I asked him to explain the rationale for this criterion. He said time spent in a setting indicated how well he enjoyed the company of his classmates and teacher. He believed that he should major in the setting that held the people he enjoyed the most. He knew to place himself in settings that attracted him and where he enjoyed the interaction with colleagues.

Actually, settings do more than attract, select, and retain occupants. To varying degrees, they re-form incumbents in predictable ways. Through the process of occupational socialization, coworkers become more alike as they perform the behaviors that constitute a job. Through the process of socialization, workers also acquire the values and attitudes of their occupational community. Initially, an individual should feel attracted to a setting and subsequently feel a sense of belongingness when working in the setting. As the context presses to shape a person's behavior, the person adapts to meet contextual requirements. Little and Joseph (2007) wrote about *mutable selves* in their social-ecological model of adaptation. They described how individuals must negotiate between personal characteristics and contextual elements in order to form meaningful goals and pursue core life projects. They gave the example of an introverted employee who performs as an enthusiastic speaker at important business meetings. After many such performances, the individual may actually seem to be more extroverted. So in selecting a setting, people do more than choose fit; they choose aspirations as to whom they wish to become through interaction with incumbents.

Determining the type of place and coworkers usually provides sufficient direction for young people to begin to explore the work world. For example, middle school students might well concentrate their exploration just on these two dimensions. However, as students mature, their interests become increasingly differentiated. Distinguishing work setting by types of place and people fails to form a complete basis for advanced exploration. Older adolescents and emerging adults must make further distinctions. So within a particular type of place and among a certain type of people, attention should focus on variations in problems and procedures. *Problem* refers to the social contribution being made, and *procedure* refers to the way that workers solve the problem. For example, if clients prefer an indoor setting with social-minded people such as teachers, they must still decide the subject and grade that they wish to teach. People interested in teaching must make many further choices about the types of students (e.g., age, ability level, socioeconomic status) whom they wish to help learn and the teaching procedures they prefer (e.g., lecture, small group, computer-assisted, independent study). The same is true for physicians and psychologists because they must select from among numerous specialties. For example, pediatricians and pathologists differ widely in problems and procedures, as do health psychologists and organizational psychologists.

VOCATIONAL INTEREST TAXONOMIES

There are so many different work settings or occupational environments that practitioners often use a simplifying taxonomy to conceptualize and summarize clients' preferred environments. The two most popular taxonomies for classifying occupational settings are ACT's (2011) World-of-Work Map and Holland's (1997) RIASEC typology of work environments. Each taxonomy provides a vocabulary of distinctions for describing settings and a knowledge system for thinking about them. ACT's World-of-Work Map offers a commonsense taxonomy. Two intersecting, bipolar axes define the map: people versus things and ideas versus data. Positioning on these two axes precisely locates occupations and college majors in one of four quadrants.

The majority of practitioners prefer to use Holland's (1997) RIASEC typology because it assumes that the people define the place. Based on the type of people who dominate a work environment, Gottfredson and Holland (1996) assigned one of six primary codes: Realistic for mechanical and outdoor settings, Investigative for scientific and analytical settings, Artistic for creative and aesthetic settings, Social for caring and educational settings, Enterprising for managerial and political settings, and Conventional for office and systematized settings. A one-letter code or designation offers, in broad strokes, a general picture of an environment. It provides an economical and simple summary of the setting and what is in it. After starting with this broad stroke, the picture can be painted in more detail by adding a second and even a third code. For example, at the college of education where I teach, Social-Realistic includes health education and vocational education, Social-Investigative includes exercise sciences and audiology, Social-Artistic includes early childhood education and special education, Social-Enterprising includes recreational management and health care administration, and Social-Conventional includes business education and community education. Adding a third letter focuses greater specificity. For example, at the same college, students enrolled in the counselor education program typically resemble Social-Artistic. But the third code distinguishes the group of students heading to work in schools (Social-Artistic-Enterprising), community agencies (Social-Artistic-Investigative), and rehabilitation bureaus (Social-Artistic-Realistic).

When assessing responses to the career story interview, practitioners may easily translate magazines, television programs, and websites into RIASEC types. For example, *People* magazine is Social, whereas *Car and Driver* is Realistic. *House* is an Investigative television show, and *This Old House* is a Realistic program. If the occupational settings that interest a client are not apparent, then practitioners may use occupational information taxonomies to generate possibilities. For example, applying the RIASEC vocabulary of distinctions to a client's interests makes it easier for practitioners to identify fitting occupations in the *Dictionary of Holland*

Occupational Codes (Gottfredson & Holland, 1996) or the *O*Net* (http://online.onetcenter.org).

SCRIPTS INTEGRATE SELF AND SETTING

Whereas the setting gives a context, a script gives a text. In the fifth element of the assessment routine, practitioners concentrate on how clients might animate a possible self in a preferred setting. After situating the self in a setting, individuals need to move the action. To identify a client's script, practitioners review a client's favorite story from a book or movie to learn which cultural tales clients reproduce and which truths reverberate in their lives. Clients adopted these scripts from the master narratives their communities provide. Living in a particular culture, individuals are born into discourses that illustrate how their shared society works and dialogues that explain their engagement with life. The stories and myths left by predecessors present archetypes of what people may do when they confront problems or encounter turning points in their lives. Thus, the traditions embedded in these master narratives are symbolic resources that a society provides to help individuals design their lives and participate as a member of that culture. Individuals use these scripts to make sense of their own experiences and clarify choices (Bohn & Berntsen, 2008).

The cultural narratives become appropriated into individual reproductions as people entwine their personal narratives around the familiar stories that saturate their sociohistorical context. The scripts come to live within them or inhabit them. This "habitus" (Bourdieu, 1977) occurs as society inculcates its objective social structures into the subjective experience of individuals. The acquired habits of meaning construction are thus a socialized subjectivity.

Career construction practitioners concentrate on the narratives from a cultural repertoire in which a client takes residence, thus staying sensitive to issues of multiculturalism and individual differences. Although each culture produces master narratives, cultures vary in the self-constituting concepts that they offer to account for experience. Autobiographical memory varies according to the cultural forms of social interaction that shape it (Fivush, 2011). Western cultures tend to shape detailed narratives that emphasize the individual's activities, thoughts, and feelings as well as personal agency. In comparison, Eastern cultures tend to shape concise narratives that emphasize the individual's actions relative to group needs and that do not diverge too far from communal norms. Knowing a culture means knowing the standard stories that the culture provides and observing how people reproduce those stories in their own lives.

Despite cultural differences, career construction practices seem especially transportable across countries. Of course, there is variation in the specific techniques. From my observations—albeit based on limited experience—weaving career construction into the saga tradition in Iceland works well, as does its use in cultures with a strong oral tradition of storytelling, such as Africa, China, and Canada's First Nations. In Australia, career construction counseling works well, yet the role model question must be phrased carefully in a country that believes it's the tall poppy that gets cut down. In Portugal, practitioners must be careful not to "blame the victim" by overemphasizing personal responsibility for their own problems. Nevertheless, with minor adjustments, career construction counseling works well in diverse countries.

Within each cultural context, practitioners must hear the tales that absorb the person and take hold of his or her life. Practitioners want to learn which narratives clients adopt to organize their aspirations and actions. Thus, practitioners inquire by asking clients to name their favorite story, in the form of either a book or a movie. After clients name the book or movie, practitioners ask the client to briefly tell the story. They want to hear the details of the story or stories that have assumed a mythic presence in a client's life. The client's personal myths become powerful and elastic metaphors that suggest how to proceed in society.

Stories hold in place the life lessons that individuals have learned, and these lessons point a way forward through ambiguity by creating scenarios that link past achievements to future initiatives. By holding onto the self in the form of a story that provides meaning and continuity, individuals are able to advance life purpose and achieve overarching goals. As a mythic enterprise, these stories contain the person and hold the self. Whereas outer setting provides an objective holding environment, an inner story provides a subjective holding environment. Career as story holds meaning, conditions feelings, shapes experience, quells anxiety, and secures space for exploration. To the extent that the career story holds individuals, they can master vocational development tasks, occupational transitions, and work traumas. During these changes, career as story functions to stabilize meaning and smooth emotional turmoil. The story enables individuals to meet uncertainties of transition with comforts recalled from the past. It can orient them to challenging transitions by meeting the disabling crisis with enabling constructs. The story allows individuals to verbalize their experiences, reflect on their meaning, and then choose how to proceed.

Practitioners know that clients have chosen some narrative from a menu of projects scripted by society (McAdams, 2008). In listening to clients tell their stories, practitioners think of a client's life as if it was a book. They want a client to tell the plot, key scenes, and turning points. The myths and metaphors in the story provide vehicles for conceptualizing the client's problems. Rather than keep spinning in the problem, concentrating on the story may solve the crisis in imagination. This process frees energy to envision options and possibilities for creative movement into the future, especially when client and practitioner view the stories as invitations, not prescriptions. The invitation is implicit because the favorite stories are not random choices.

The practitioner's job is to show how the story plot may resolve the current dilemma. People are attracted to books in which a major character experiences problems similar to their own. Clients' favorite stories tell of their own situation. Moreover, a favorite story singles out a script for moving forward. Clients find encouragement in how the script portrays the problem and how to cope with it. The story's script comforts clients as they learn how another person resolved a similar problem. In short, the favorite story provides a script for living that the client finds especially useful. Kenneth Burke (1938), a preeminent literary critic, called stories "equipment for living." Stories offer individuals a means for solving the puzzle that they face, and these solutions can propel them forward. For example, a transgendered client explained that her favorite book, *Stranger in a Strange Land* (Heinlein, 1961), taught her to study the culture she lived in and encouraged her to work to change it. The story lit a beacon that drew her forward. As 19th-century philosopher and educator Bronson Alcott once profoundly remarked about *The Pilgrim's Progress,* "the book gave me to myself . . . I thought and spoke through it. It was my most efficient teacher" (quoted in Brooks, 2006).

Favorite stories can remain alive since childhood, similar to the durability of role models. For example, the singer Dolly Parton named as her favorite book *The Little Engine That Could,* and she can (Parton, 2010). A lawyer, late in his career and looking to make retirement decisions, told his practitioner that whenever he felt down or defeated, he went to WalMart and purchased a copy of *The Little Engine That Could.* Like Dolly Parton, he drew great inspiration and comfort from the tale. The showman Walt Disney never forgot the Uncle Remus stories of his childhood (Harris, 1881). Ernest Hemingway (1935) remained enthralled by Mark Twain's *Huckleberry Finn.* Following Huck's script, Hemingway and his alter ego Nick Adams wanted to find out about men and how they lived together.

Although some clients report long-held scripts, other clients have a more recent favorite story. They have moved to a new script to address a problem their old story could not comprehend. So some clients tell of a favorite story from today, maybe the book *The Shack* (Young, 2007) or the movie *The Blind Side* (Hancock, 2009). The ease of adopting a new favorite story enables individuals to be flexible. Typically, the role model remains the same, yet now it appears in a new story. The engagement of the old character with a new story accounts for both the constancy and change seen in lives. On occasion, I have asked clients to trace their favorite stories across childhood, adolescence, emerging adulthood, and middle adulthood. This exercise reveals the truth in Thoreau's (1854/1992) observation about reading: "How many a man has dated a new era in his life from the reading of a book! The book exists for us perchance which will explain our miracles and reveal new ones" (p. 56). To see an example of how particular books become important during different eras in a life cycle, readers may watch an episode from the Borders bookstore series called "Shelf Indulgence" (Borders, n.d.) in which authors and artists describe their favorite books. The actress Jamie Lee Curtis tells how as a child the important book was *Go, Dog, Go!;* as an adolescent it became *King Rat;* as a young adult it was *Shogun;* and at midlife it became *The English Patient.* After describing how each book influenced her, Curtis ends by saying, "OK, I think that's me" (Borders, n.d.). Applying story sequence analysis (Arnold, 1962) to the book plots, one might speculate about a progression from developing relationships, to feeling isolated and struggling with authority, then understanding the other, and eventually reconnecting.

STORIES: EQUIPMENT FOR LIVING

The adolescent Sigmund Freud provides another good example of finding a solution to one's problem in literature. Freud (1915) once wrote, "In the realm of fiction we find the plurality of lives which we need" (p. 291). The novelist Cervantes provided Freud with both a role model and a script. Similar to Cervantes, Freud suffered disillusionment regarding his father. Initially Freud viewed his father as a powerful and wise man. When his father told young Sigmund how he had shown humiliating weakness in the face of anti-Semitic ruffians, Sigmund was painfully disappointed and disillusioned (Jones, 1953, pp. 7–22). Freud found a model for dealing with this type of disillusionment in Cervantes, who had also witnessed weakness in his father. Freud identified with Cervantes's ideals and dedicated himself to the pursuit of self-knowledge. From the novel *Don Quixote,* Freud learned that a hero must become "victorious over himself, which is the highest kind of victory" (cf. *Don Quixote* Part II, Chapter 72). Freud crafted a career in which he could become victorious over himself and help other people become heroes and heroines in their own lives. Using the script of Cervantes's novella *Colloquy of Dogs* (Cervantes, 1613/1976), from which Freud appropriated the name Cipión for himself, Freud learned to problematize rational thinking (Kinney, 2007). Cervantes cast the novella in the form of a dialogue in which Berganza tells his life story to Cipión, who listens as well as interrupts to comment, criticize, and philosophize—a prelude to what would become the axis of psychoanalysis and counseling (Riley, 1994).

A client's synopsis of a favorite story unifies the self as portrayed in role models and the social niche situated by favorite magazines or television shows. It integrates disparate elements of life into a dynamic whole that links personal commitments to recognizable roles in the social world. For example, the young woman who wanted to free herself from her mother explained that her favorite story was about a girl who goes on a voyage by herself, and this is what she herself did later in a job that had her travel the country. A man about to change careers to become an archivist reported his favorite book to be *Fahrenheit 451*, a story about people who prevent the burning of books (Bradbury, 1987). In short, at this point in the assessment practitioners begin to compose a tentative identity narrative for a client in which the self enters a preferred setting to enact a script that leads to a life-enhancing career, particularly one that addresses the preoccupations embedded in early recollections. A goal of counseling will be to have clients edit and then adopt this storyline as a form of biographical agency with which to deal with tasks, transitions, and traumas.

In addition to linking self to setting, the script should also be tied to the earliest recollection. Recall that a life portrait shows the self as possessing the characteristics needed to deal with the preoccupations in the early recollections. The script puts that self into action. It shows the storyline of how the client turns passive to active and, in so doing, solves the self and resolves the preoccupation. Recall that the narrative paradigm in career construction theory has a particular approach to composing a macronarrative. It traces a transformation from how the person has been influenced by the problem to how the person can influence the problem. It portrays active mastery as the client reauthoring a story. At its most succinct, in just a few words it tells how a client has gone from problem to solution.

For example, a female client told a story of being the youngest child, a girl among four older brothers, who believed that each day she had to prove herself to be their equal. Her life theme became apparent as she told her tales—she had moved from "prove" to "improve." Eventually she was able to transform her preoccupation with proving how well she did into a focus on what she did each day to improve herself. The dialogue discussed how she now competed not with others but with her last performance as she worked to hone her talents and enact a career. During counseling, she was in the process of turning her strength into a social contribution by entering the ministry to help other people improve their lives. In this occupation she would live a line from Emily Dickinson's (1960) poem "The Province of the Saved": "The Province of the Saved / Should be the Art —

to save / Through Skill obtained in Themselves" (p. 539). Connecting past negative experiences to current strengths and future opportunities prompts a process of self-transformation. Narrative reconstruction of this transformation, or what McAdams (2008) called a *redemption script*, helps individuals to work through transitions. Redemptive restructuring of narratives encourages and enables self-change and career transition (McLean & Breen, 2009).

In many instances, the life portrait should use the script to vocalize the client's dreams in a way that encourages him or her to reenter the world. The script is a unifying message that compels a choice that is simultaneously predetermined and unpredictable. The script is the précis of a story to transport the client into the future. This is also the place to insert and discuss emotional issues so as to prepare the client for future struggles. Consider the favorite story of an African American graduate student. He liked the movie *Higher Learning* because it tells the story of a college freshman who perseveres through tribulations to become a man of purpose (Singleton, 1995).

DECONSTRUCTION

A caveat about individuals as bearers of culture must be stated here. Cultural scripts articulate dominant discourses that offer a supportive scheme for identity construction by focusing on a way of moving forward in life. Influential stories come to be seen as canonical in a culture. Despite their usefulness, the cultural canon limits the range of possible selves and styles of living that individuals may adopt. Cultural scripts do so by forcing individuals to adhere to cultural assumptions, behavioral norms, gender stereotypes, and social inequalities. They become dominant or master narratives as they subsume differences and contradictions, restrict and restrain people, support the power structure, and define who matters and how.

Practitioners must open such closed texts so as not to defer or deflect the authority of clients in scripting their own journey. Professional ethics require that practitioners help clients recognize the confining and restricting aspects of their favorite stories as cultural products that may distort their lives. Practitioners must always think carefully about how a client's micronarratives might be deconstructed to reveal self-limiting ideas and cultural barriers concealed in the stories. They may deconstruct the story by discussing what the story overlooks, omits, forgets, or inadequately addresses. Deconstruction seeks to undo a story's uncritical domination over a client's thinking, not destroy the story. As appropriate, practitioners encourage clients to expose assumptions and question the certainties of their favorite story by highlighting inconsistencies, challenging dichotomies, and flattening hierarchies. Yet more than recognition is needed. Practitioners should encourage clients to confront the impact of these cultural distortions in their own lives. This process leads directly to examining what clients, as the authority on their own lives, believe should be done next.

To become more informed about scripts and to practice recognizing them, practitioners might study literary criticism. Although not to be taken at face value, some critics claim there are only five different scripts used in all stories. Holland's (1997) RIASEC typology concentrates on six scripts. For example, the Realistic script goes from weak to strong, the Artistic script goes from inhibited to expressive, and the Enterprising script goes from ignored to noticed. Practitioners who wish to study fundamental scripts might read two books. Polti (1916) condensed all script patterns into 36 dramatic situations (e.g., ambition, revolt, remorse, revenge, disaster, loss, deliverance, madness). He did this to help writers generate plots, yet his work also may help career construction practitioners recognize the structure of clients' scripts. In a similar vein, Propp (1968) examined 100 Russian fairy tales to identify five possible characters (e.g., the hero, helper, villain) and 31 possible actions (e.g., trickery, struggle, pursuit). Even more directly relevant to studying career construction counseling are discussions of favorite books published by prominent individuals. Practitioners may start with two general audience books. The first, titled *You've Got to Read This Book* (Canfield & Hendricks, 2006), consists of 55 people describing the book that changed their lives. The second, *The Play That Changed My Life* (Hodges, 2009), consists of 21 playwrights and actors describing how plays and theater gave them their calling.

CONSIDER THE NEXT EPISODE

By now, the script for directing the next scene in the occupational plot should be clear. So attention turns to naming an incident or episode that will get things moving. In this sixth element in the assessment routine, practitioners consider what may stir action by examining the client's motto. Typically the motto is stated as a short expression of a guiding principle or rule of conduct. A favorite saying expresses the words of wisdom that clients have for themselves. As a call to action, the epigram offers encouragement that clients give to themselves in suggesting an episode that will move the plot to the next scenario. As a premonitory truth, it points the way to the next scene in the occupational plot.

Knowing a self, setting, and script is sufficient for the practitioner, but it is not sufficient for the client. Clients seek counseling because they are stuck or have writer's block in advancing the script to the next chapter in their autobiography. This is precisely when hearing their own motto helps propel action. The motto is a command from the story's director (i.e., themselves) in which they express the best advice they have for themselves. A motto encapsulates and expresses what clients intend to do to start moving again. This intention and motivation, repeated many times during a life, may become the slogan that a client uses whenever trouble appears. In this sense, the Roman Emperor Constantine's motto has become the motto of mottoes. Constantine prepared himself for battles with the Greek motto *In hoc signo vinces*—"With this sign you shall conquer." That is the essence of a motto—namely, a saying with which individuals may conquer their troubles. However, clients frequently need assistance to recognize the intentions stated in their motto.

Each client possesses an inner wisdom with which to guide himself or herself. The deep meaning of a personal truth encapsulated in a motto becomes evident against the backdrop of the client's current situation. Often the saying directly and succinctly provides the wisdom clients sought in entering counseling. Practitioners should make this explicit by carefully comparing the motto to the client's response to how counseling could be useful to them. Practitioners may help clients appreciate how their motto actually provides the directions they seek. After all, it states their best advice to themselves. It is a form of autotherapy in which clients repeatedly tell themselves what they must do to advance their story to a new chapter and, in so doing, become more complete. This self-organizing wisdom embodies self-help at its finest.

CALLS TO ACTION

The Danish memoirist Isak Dinesen (1979) wrote a chapter on mottoes, one that explains how they function as self-help. In the chapter, she reviewed the mottos that she adopted through her life. She began with her first motto, one adopted as part of identity crystallization. She wrote, "I think that it must have been at the age of fifteen . . . that the rich possibilities consolidated into one, and I chose the first real motto of my youth. 'It is necessary to sail, it is not necessary to live'" (p. 5). Dinesen wrote, "I steered my course by it with unswerving confidence" (p. 5). Variations of this motto served her later in life: "Often in difficulties, never afraid" and "Still I am unconquered" (p. 4). Dinesen's mottoes told her what she must do next.

Most clients know implicitly what they must do next. Effective counseling requires more than just having clients make that knowledge explicit. The goal is to have clients hear their own wisdom and examine how to apply it directly to the problems they brought to counseling. It sounds simple, and it is. Nevertheless, it is profound. The process of making clients listen to their own advice reinforces clients' authority in authoring their own lives. It builds confidence because clients realize that the answers to their questions are within themselves. Instead of being an expert on the client's life, the practitioner functions as witness who validates and elaborates a client's intuitive solutions. In a cultural narrative relevant to this aspect of counseling and psychotherapy, the *Wizard of Oz* informs readers that Dorothy had within her all along the power to return home, just by clicking her heels together and making it so (LeRoy & Fleming, 1939). The message of the story is made explicit in a dialogue at the end of the movie version of the story:

Dorothy: Oh, will you help me? Can you help me?

Glenda: You do not need to be helped any longer. You've always had the power to go back to Kansas.

Dorothy: I have?

Scarecrow: Then why didn't you tell her before?

Glenda: Because she wouldn't have believed me. She had to learn it for herself.

As Dorothy realizes, the solution is not somewhere over the rainbow, but within oneself.

In listening to a client's motto, practitioners must connect the advice to the problem with which the client struggles. This turns the saying into a call for action that may resolve the problem at hand. It might provide a helpful example now if readers identify their own favorite saying and reflect upon how that saying relates to their life overall and to the challenges they now face. A woman forced by her husband not to enter the workforce said, "Break the ties that bind." A woman who hesitated to pursue her dream job said, "Life is not life until you live it; love is not love until you give it." A college student being pressured to major in premed by his parents said, "Do not succumb to the expectations of others." A student rejected from her preferred graduate school said, "When a door closes, a window opens." A medical student forced to accept a residency far down his list said, "Do what you can with what you have." A student who had just failed an important examination said, "If it's going to be, it's up to me." A musician who suffered from chronic depression said, "All suffering is some measure of love seeking to be born into this world." A poet who suffered from a mood disorder said, "One still must have chaos in oneself to give birth to a dancing star" (Nietzsche, 1954, p. 5). Facing a difficult yet important midcareer change, a woman executive said, "There came a time when the risk to remain tight in the bud was more painful than the risk it took to blossom" (undocumented, but typically attributed to Anaïs Nin). A blind client said, "Give it a go" and quoted her hero Stevie Wonder as saying, "Impossible is not acceptable." A lawyer who felt self-conscious about her material success and had started to donate time and treasure to the less fortunate said, "Live simply so that others may simply live."

Career construction practitioners return to the motto several times during the final 10 minutes of counseling. They run the motto's meaning backward and forward to ensure that clients hear the advice that they have for themselves. It is critical for them to understand that the answers they sought from the practitioner were actually within themselves all the time. These are the exact words they need to carry with them as they leave the office. Their own motto will propel them forward. Consider the example of a young Hispanic woman who sought consultation about which prelaw major would fit her best. It soon became obvious that she wanted to become a psychologist but was afraid to tell her father for fear of breaking his heart. Her favorite saying was, "If you are what you do, and you don't, then you aren't." Playing that motto backward and forward in her career story helped her declare a major in psychology. She eventually became a professor of psychology and teaches law and ethics to psychology students.

PLOT A FUTURE SCENARIO

The seventh step in the assessment protocol finds practitioners brainstorming about academic majors or occupational titles that may engage the client. Having considered a client's occupational plot and career theme in the previous steps, possible scenarios are usually self-evident. However, to expand the list practitioners may turn to a more formal procedure. At this point, person–occupation translation materials devised to implement the classic matching model of vocational guidance are useful, particularly those based on personality systematics such as Holland's (1997) typology of work environments. For example, applying Holland's RIASEC language to a client's favorite setting, practitioners can translate magazines, television shows, or websites into an occupational code. Then they may find those codes in the *Dictionary of Holland Occupational Codes* (Gottfredson & Holland, 1996) to generate a list of fitting occupations. For example, one client reported that she read regularly *Us, Star,* and *Soap Opera Digest.* Her favorite television shows were two soap operas, *The Young and the Restless* and *The Bold and the Beautiful,* along with *Survivor* and *Oz.* The magazines about celebrities and soap operas present Social environments. The television shows *Survivor,* about endurance and physical skill, and *Oz,* set in a maximum security prison, present Realistic environments. In *Oz,* many of the plots occur in an experimental unit that emphasizes rehabilitation and learning social responsibility. So when combined, the client's responses sum into a preference for Social-Realistic environments in which we find, to name a few, police officers, coaches, physical therapists, midwives, podiatrists, and rehabilitation counselors. After earning a degree in rehabilitation counseling, the client began work as a job development specialist at a vocational rehabilitation agency, an occupation and setting that fit her Social-Realistic preferences.

In comparison, a client majoring in English read *The Utne Reader, Poets and Writers, International Literary Quarterly, Archeology,* and *National Geographic* for "adventure, mystery, and imagination." These magazines signal a strong preference for Artistic environments, followed by interest in Investigative environments. So when combined, the client's responses sum into a preference for the Artistic-Investigative environments in which we find, to name a few, writers, editors, set designers, illustrators, and architects. Today, the client works as a copywriter for a magazine in Australia, while in his free time he edits and publishes a poetry quarterly.

The eighth and final step element in the assessment protocol has practitioners formulate a response to the client's initial request for consultation. It may not be, and often is not, for suggestions about educational majors to pursue or occupations to choose. It usually is about clarifying some issue that makes them hesitant about moving forward. For example, a recent client said, "I do not know what I want to become. Am I wasting my time in this college?" In the end she clearly explained that midway through her training to become a community counselor, she had decided to go to law school. She originally said that she was thinking of quitting the counseling program. At the end of counseling, she admitted having never seriously considered quitting. The one-session consultation had been useful to her in seeing that she always wanted to become an advocate for people without a voice. Now she saw her counseling training as giving her skills she could use later in a career as a civil rights lawyer. No longer did she view the program as a waste of time; linked to her commitment to a life of advocacy, it had become an investment in her own self-growth and professional development. She knew this all along yet needed to narrate it with more continuity, coherence, and comprehensibility.

8

Counseling for
Career Construction

Having conducted the eight-step assessment protocol, practitioners prepare to compose a portrait that depicts a lifetime of experiences from a new perspective on career. Practitioners draw a life portrait that transforms little stories into a grand narrative that expresses identity and provides a superordinate view that comprehends the current transition and envisions future positions. Practitioners want to use the composition to help clients understand their lives by deploying past experiences to consider future choices. They do so by using the career theme to extend the occupational plot into the future. So in composing a life portrait, they reconstruct the past in ways meant to anticipate the future and prompt action.

To compose a life portrait, the practitioner reconstructs the client's micronarratives into a first draft of a macronarrative and then eventually coconstruct with him or her a final version authorized by the client. In portraying a life as a work of art, practitioners craft a word portrait that highlights the client's distinctive features in relation to important career themes and emerging extensions of the occupational plot. This means writing a life in a way that configures the small stories from the career story interview into a large story that highlights the abstract theme winnowed from the concrete stories. As is discussed following the presentation of general principles for life writing, the sequence of topics in the career story interview foreshadows the large story.

GENERAL PRINCIPLES

Five general principles guide writing a life portrait. First, in composing the identity narrative, practitioners should give the best possible account of a client's life at that particular time. They should infuse the portrait with character and values, thereby raising the dignity and significance of the life. As far as reasonable, they strive for a jubilant portrayal of the life in progress. In all cases, they bend the character arc in a hopeful direction and clarify dreams by articulating them. For example, one client reveled in his own movement from being a teenage wisecracker to becoming an adult who shared his wisdom. Practitioners use the weight of past experiences to confirm the present poetics of personhood and future politics of career construction. And they always tell the large story in a definitive way that makes it stay told, similar to a picture that finally stays on the wall with the right adhesive.

Second, practitioners compose the narrative in a way that opens possibilities. Many client stories lend themselves to different metaphorical retellings. The life portrait should highlight the metaphors spoken by the client. This figurative language usually plants seeds of possibilities from which new options may grow (Neimeyer, 2004a). Thus, the metaphors should reach widely to create openness and deeply to create significance. In addition to using a client's metaphors, practitioners should use the client's vocabulary and phrases as much as possible. Letting a client's life speak for itself, in its own way and with its own words, promotes comprehension and credibility. As necessary, practitioners may use new language to push back constraints and open more space for living. Recall the Russian girl who became puzzled about the word *privacy*. Learning that word opened a new space in her life. In addition to providing new language, practitioners can open lines of movement by confronting false dichotomies and disjunctive expectations that constrain life. People can see only what language allows them to see, so adding a word or changing "either/or" to "both/and" may propel action in new directions.

Third, the life portrait should focus on animating themes that extend the occupational plot. Clarification and change in understanding occur for clients when a new unity reorganizes a previous configuration of the meaning system. Practitioners emphasize career themes to reorder occupational plots in ways that enable reintegration of self, renewal of identity, and revitalization of life. If one views a life portrait as a tapestry, then the pattern or theme can be likened to the vibrant anchor thread that holds together diverse threads. Practitioners highlight thematic patterning by emphasizing the unifying argument or salient idea reflected in seemingly disparate events. A life portrait must emphasize progressive realization of wholeness by showing trends in the past carried steadily forward into the present. Remember, emplotment arranges stories in a sequence directed toward a conclusion. Accordingly, the larger story or macronarrative strings together small stories along an anchor thread to highlight the logic underlying the progression of development and elaboration of meaning.

In patterning an identity narrative, practitioners do well to take a hermeneutic stance in drawing the client's stories backward and forward as well as inward and outward along the thematic anchor thread. Usually, this is easily done because client microstories tend to be repetitious, with core themes recurring throughout the micronarratives. Similar to novelists, practitioners try to show that a certain underlying unity exists just below the surface of stories. Life is not a collection of disparate events; clients must wrestle with the theme, not isolated facts. The career theme should explain purpose and meaning while justifying the person's most distinctive commitments and investments. The narrative identity follows the thematic thread by frequently repeating the motif explicitly and avoids detours into facts and information that may be interesting yet not particularly relevant.

Fourth, the life portrait must be credible, comprehensible, coherent, and continuous as it explains the career themes that shape clients' deliberations and predispose them to certain actions. Clients must see themselves through the portrait if the portrait is to see them through their current transition. Portraits must be credible for clients to accept them. Logical and systematic development of the identity narrative interspersed with consistent, corroborating details enhances credibility. Nevertheless, practitioners should not pursue a consistent line of reasoning at the expense of authenticity. A life portrait, as appropriate, should include ambiguities, contradictions, and multiplicities as they are present in the life. Divergent definitions and expectations that extend in different directions than the main theme may open new possibilities. Although a life portrait may include complexities, a comprehensible portrait clarifies each part, a coherent portrait unifies the parts, and a continuous portrait shows a progressive realization of wholeness.

Fifth and finally, practitioners must be disciplined and controlled in interpreting the meaning of client stories as they compose a life portrait. Career construction practitioners help clients to scrutinize implicit meanings and elaborate wider dimensions of meaning. They should never stoop to explain a client's individuality through facile formulations of modern psychology. The truth is too complex to be decoded by a practitioner. Career construction practitioners respect clients' dignity by serving as witnesses who participate in the coconstruction of meaning and understanding as clients make sense of their lives. In the career construction model, practitioners reconstruct clients' narratives from a career story interview into a life portrait, and then with clients they coconstruct meaning through transformative conversations. Through the process of coconstruction, clients contemplate the themes highlighted in the life portrait to produce a new, jointly authored account (Schafer, 1983).

In reconstruction of client micronarratives into a macronarrative, practitioners emphasize artistic and empirical inferences over interpretations. They do not typically seek to interpret symbols or make psychodynamic formulations. They prefer an aesthetic interpretation, similar to finding beauty in a painting or unity in a symphony. It is better to emphasize the context for choices, not an explanation of a choice. Providing context for a turning point helps a client to understand the text of the current transition. Practitioners strive to comprehend clients' meanings and intentions, not impose them. Although some practitioners would prefer to avoid interpretation altogether, they cannot. Their responses to and reinforcement of elements of client stories already begin to shape meaning. Interpretation is not performed by a practitioner alone; the relationship contributes to it as clients select the stories to tell and how they tell them. When it comes time to compose a life portrait, interpretation begins in simply selecting the incidents, metaphors, and words that will become the identity narrative. Clients guide practitioners in this interpretive process. During a career story interview, practitioners should have prompted clients to interpret themselves by frequently directing client reflection in asking, "What does that mean?" "How do you see it?" and "How do you put those together?" In reconstructing a draft of a life portrait, practitioners emphasize these client self-interpretations, adding their own subtle, sensible, and sensitive interpretations.

To ensure that the interpretations are ethical as well as aesthetic, career construction practitioners rigorously and skeptically examine systematically gathered data. Because practitioners listen *for* a story, not *to* a story, their interpretations stem from an epistemological perspective, empirical theory, and systematic framework. They use career construction theory to recognize themes, select details, connect stories, and organize a unified whole. In doing so, they make subtle interpretations that lie just under the surface of client micronarratives. And they form them as observations of a whole made from a distance, something clients cannot do for themselves. Because practitioners use both reasoning and intuition to compose a life portrait, they must be aware of their biases and skeptical of the outcomes produced by their assessment. Having reconstructed client small stories into a larger story, practitioners must be open to misunderstandings and surprises as together with clients they revise the portrait and coconstruct an identity narrative that the client authorizes. To learn more about composing life portraits, practitioners may consult *The Art and Science of Portraiture: A New Approach to Qualitative Research* (Lawrence-Lightfoot & Hoffman Davis, 1997) and *Career Counseling: A Narrative Approach* (Cochran, 1997).

In sum, the five general principles for composing an identity narrative enjoin practitioners to prepare the best possible version, open new possibilities, avoid facile interpretations, concentrate on themes, and include complexities that explain constancy and change. Practitioners strive to compose a life portrait that holds the client's dreams and provides

guidance in times of trouble. The macronarrative portrays, with an enduring vitality, a fresh and figurative picture of the client's identity, one that
should both inform and inspire the client. Having surveyed the general
principles of composing a life portrait, attention now turns to the specific
routine practitioners may adopt in composing the narrative.

STRUCTURE THE COMPOSITION

A systematic routine guides composing a life portrait. The customary course
of composition calls for six topics, with each topic leading to the next to
build momentum. For most clients, the topics each require a few sentences,
whereas for other clients they may each require a paragraph. The first topic
provides a panorama. Following the aesthetic principle used by movie direc-
tors, the portraitist sets up the vista before taking the individual into the
scene under construction and finally the moment of commitment.

Topic 1: Preoccupation

The first section of the life portrait should meet the dictum stated by
Thurber (1956) in his fable about lemmings: "All men [people] should
strive to learn before they die what they are running from, and to, and
why" (p. 174). To begin novelizing a client's life, practitioners look to his
or her early recollections to identify the core issues, origin of career
themes, and base of the character arc. In presenting the identity narrative
to a client, discussing the preoccupations in the early recollections makes
a smooth transition. The early recollections were the final topic in the
career story interview, so making them the first topic in presenting the
identity narrative flows well. Practitioners search for the main idea by
identifying the preoccupation or problem repeatedly faced, as illustrated
in the early recollections. Then they ask themselves questions such as,
What questions will the narrative answer? How should the life portrait
begin? How should it be told? What complications and conflicts are
involved? What endings are fruitful?

In a book about "reading your life path in literature," the psychotherapist and literary critic Allan Hunter (2008) provided a good illustration of

life as repeatedly revisiting a core issue. Hunter's analysis of J. K. Rowling's *Harry Potter* series of novels illustrates how individuals keep returning to the same basic struggle throughout their lives. Progression occurs when each time individuals return to their preoccupation, they enter it at a deeper level and with more complexity. In each novel or academic year, Harry Potter accrues new skills and more personal power. Yet it is not power and egoism that Harry Potter pursues with purpose. It is love and loyalty that are revisited and developed in each novel. Harry's story, like all of our own stories, becomes increasingly clear over the years without ever losing a sense of mystery. As succinctly stated by the poet Edna St. Vincent Millay, "It's not true that life is one damn thing after another; it's one damn thing over and over" (Famous Poets and Poems, n.d.). So practitioners begin a life portrait by stating the "one damn thing" that a client faces repeatedly and what it means to that client. This approach to portraiture seeks to convey the client's emotional essence by investing that personal meaning with the client's own deepest feelings.

The day I was writing this page, I read a story in *The New York Times* that stated singer/songwriter Carly Simon "has always been driven by her life's narrative" (Clifford, 2009, p. C1). At age 64, Simon was quoted in an article by Stephanie Clifford (2009) as saying, "I want to be somebody who faces things and who doesn't get stepped on because I've been stepped on too much in my life and I don't want my self-esteem to suffer" (p. C8). In writing about the themes present in their discussion of Simon's lawsuit against Starbucks Coffee Company for mismanagement of a recording project, Clifford identified Simon's life themes as "broken trust, men misbehaving, women trying to recover" (p. C1). Simon had written a note to Starbucks's chief executive, Howard Schultz, in which she stated, "Howard, Fraud is the creation of Faith/And then the betrayal" (p. C8). Clifford highlighted the continuing personal meaning represented in Simon's first hit record, *That's the Way I've Always Heard It Should Be*.

Topic 2: Self

Stating the preoccupation is followed by describing how the client has built a self to manage that preoccupation. This self-construction has led to a character that possesses all the qualities needed to meet that "one damn thing." Implied, yet maybe not yet explicitly stated, in the life portrait could be the idea that the issue the client brought to counseling is that "one damn thing" in different garb. The practitioner as portraitist should be sure to emphasize the lifelong importance and current usefulness of key qualities that the client has incorporated into the self.

Topic 3: Setting

A third section explains the social niche and preferred environment in which the client wishes to situate the self. The life portrait should include several examples and details concerning how well the self has been constructed to operate in the preferred settings. Practitioners should also be sensitive to the client's interests in different settings. Some clients have highly differentiated interests that concentrate on one type of setting—say, the Social world. However, other clients, although still differentiated, focus on two or three types of settings. For them, different contexts evoke different meanings. Practitioners must discuss the different identities that a client shows in different settings yet still bring forward the pattern common to all favored settings. With clients who show undifferentiated interests—that is, some interest in almost every setting—the life portrait must show how flexibility and adaptability pattern their lives.

Topic 4: Script

The fourth section explicitly unites self and setting by recounting a script. In articulating the client's script, it is useful to select phrases that the client used to tell his or her favorite story. These phrases should describe clearly how the self wants to operate on the stage of work, and maybe even life. The presentation of the script must highlight the transformative scenes that address recurrent themes. It should also state the client's credo— namely, the idea that is served by his or her life. An example of the power of this came to me in hearing a practitioner say to her client, "I think that is why you became a detective—to figure out your family's mystery."

Topic 5: Advice

The next section in a life portrait explains to clients that they sought counseling at the end of an act. There has been an intermission, and now it is time for an episode to begin the next act. There must be some continuity and coherence in the story line or both the lead character and the audience will be lost. The author—that is, the client—must give some direction to himself or herself as lead actor. This is the deeper meaning of the favorite saying. It is the direction that the self-as-author gives to the self-as-actor. The practitioner must make it clearly relevant to resuming the script after the intermission with a new act that extends the occupational plot. The practitioner should repeat the saying several times during the remainder of the session, drawing its profound meaning inward, outward, backward, and forward.

Topic 6: Future Scenario

The final section restates the client's reason for seeking consultation and then relates that reason to the other sections of the life portrait. Practitioners intend to demystify the client's presenting problem by offering a plausible understanding of it. In this concluding section, practitioners explain how that "one damn thing" may have reappeared in the occupational plot, how the career theme drafts a future scenario to extend the plot in a fitting direction, and how the favorite saying describes what the client proposes to do next. The section should conceptualize clients' character as a solution to problems in growing up and their interests as a means of turning tension to intention, problem to opportunity, and preoccupation to occupation. Vocational interests should be presented as enabling constructs that help clients to address disabling tasks, transitions, and traumas.

The portrait should afford clients an opportunity to understand the origin of their interests as well as their current meaning and significance in a way that makes the future conceivable and attainable. The section may include a fictive truth for the client's life. That personal mythology may be epitomized in a character arc. As the aesthetic principle that structures an identity narrative, the arc traces how clients have turned problems into strengths, and then strengths into occupations and social contributions. Recall examples of clients going from fear to fortitude, proving to improving, and wisecracker to wise man. Finally, this last section of the life portrait suggests a way forward, a new chapter in which the client plays the role of hero or heroine in his or her own life story.

Before the second meeting with the client, practitioners should review the life portrait as a whole. In examining the identity narrative, they should avoid getting stuck in the dichotomy of right versus wrong. The portrait must have a *pragmatic viability* that is subjectively useful to the client, rather than a *logical validity* that is objectively right (Neimeyer, 1995). Accordingly, practitioners review the life portrait to determine whether it might be useful to the client. Two different life portraits could be equally useful. Thus, practitioners should ask themselves how useful this identity narrative would be to the client in easing self-exploration, prompting occupational exploration, and fostering career decision making. Having settled on an initial life portrait, practitioners prepare to begin counseling with the client. This could be in the second half of the initial hour or in a second session.

NARRATE THE PORTRAIT TO THE CLIENT

The second meeting in career counseling begins by asking clients, "What has become clearer since we last met?" (cf. Neimeyer, 2009, p. 81). Practitioners follow this question by asking clients if they wish to add anything to what they said during the first session. Practitioners then move to a restatement of how clients thought counseling might be useful to them, especially highlighting areas of puzzlement as a prelude to the life portrait.

Practitioners begin counseling by narrating to the client the draft of the life portrait that they have reconstructed from the client's microstories. They retell a client's stories about how he or she has fashioned an original way of living, intensifying the theme and dramatizing the character arc as they proceed. They attempt to coax alive the client as the author of his or her own story, not just the actor. In so doing, practitioners seek to affect a more reflexive sense of self by encouraging the client to move fluidly back and forth between his or her internal view of self and the self-as-other portrayed in the identity narrative. The portrait must be authentic in attending to the claims of the client's particular story. However, the life portrait is not a proclamation of fact from a practitioner; rather, it is tentative truth, open to question and revision. Practitioners wish to use it as a resource for dialogue and deliberation in taking clients on a journey to discover what is true for them. Narrating back to clients the career themes that hold their lives informs clients about what is at stake and inspires them to make choices that resonate with their spirit.

Lifting the portrait up for contemplation and reflection is a means for clients to better see themselves and understand how they are living their lives. Practitioners should encourage clients to enter the composition, wander and wonder a bit, and then exit with enlightened awareness. Self-reflection in a quest for wholeness allows clients to derive a greater sense of meaning from their circumstances. In thinking about the portrait, people can come to know it, analyze it, learn from it, and change it. This reflection should be well timed, but not time consuming. In the middle of a challenging dislocation, they need to reflect on the event while holding the life portrait in mind. More time-consuming reflection may come later if they so choose.

To enhance the client's ability to explore the meaning of the identity portrait, practitioners must narrate it in a clear and crisp manner. This simple and direct narration encourages the client to engage in a conscious effort to both fully acknowledge and then reflectively process the tentative macronarrative presented by the practitioner. To the untrained ear, this simple and direct recital may sound like interpretations from the practitioner's perspective. Nevertheless, on closer listening one recognizes that most of the interpretations merely reconstruct what the client has already said. Practitioners are scrupulous in using as many client constructions and self-interpretations as possible. They repeat phrases the client has used and draw out the implications therein. In particular, they emphasize the headlines from the early recollections and the script of the favorite story. If they need to add their own interpretations, they do so reluctantly and sparingly, always announcing them as their own conjectures for the client to accept or reject. The client is the author of his or her own life and the only one with the authority to say what it means.

Practitioners must ensure that clients recognize their career themes and occupational plots. Once in a great while, a client does not readily recognize a life portrait that a practitioner has reconstructed and thus is not prepared to coconstruct a revision. For example, I did a public demonstration with a volunteer who after listening to my reconstruction of her identity narrative said, "I never thought of myself in that way. I have to go home and think about it." Immediately, three of her coworkers in turn said that they were surprised because the life portrait expressed exactly how they saw her. They even provided specific examples to validate the life portrait. Nevertheless, the client needed more time to reflect. Fortunately, we had taped the consultation so, if she chose, she could hear it again and refine it to her satisfaction or discard it. The diverging perspectives on the life portrait demonstrate the difference between pragmatic viability for the client versus the logical validity to her audience. More typical is the reaction of an articulate client who explained that the life portrait was very different from the interest inventory that he had recently taken. He said,

> I believe that my interest inventory results were an example of wish fulfillment, describing the person that I thought I should be rather than who I really am. As I was introduced to the "me" emerging from the life portrait, I said, "Yes, that's me! That's who I am!"

Obviously, in narrating life portraits to clients, practitioners must look for evidence that clients recognize themselves in their portraits and take possession of who they are. Although client verbal expressions of agreement are fine, they are abstractions. Career construction practitioners prefer to watch for concrete bodily expressions of felt recognition, what Dreikurs (1967) called a *recognition reflex*. When clients recognize themselves in their portraits, they emit an involuntary, spontaneous reaction such as smile, tear, blush, or laugh. To me, felt bodily experience indicates that the client resonates with the portrait. As body language experts often proclaim, "the body never lies."

If for some reason the practitioner needs to reinforce a client's recognition of the career theme, then he or she may use one or two techniques to deepen the recognition. One technique is to identify examples of how clients' patterns are expressed in their present behavior, preferably during the last 5 minutes or if not, in some things they said or did during the career story interview. The second technique is to ask clients to cite an example of something they have done during the past week that expresses their pattern. Having heard their life portrait, it is time for clients to use their authority to revise and enrich the identity narrative with greater depth, complexity, and wisdom.

REVISE THE PORTRAIT TOGETHER

A first goal in narrating the life portrait to clients is to have them consider the macronarrative reconstructed by the practitioner. Thinking about this life telling and reflecting on it typically lead to the client editing the identity narrative. Thus, the next activity finds the client and practitioner collaborating in coconstructing an even more credible and authentic narrative. This involves amendments that correct mistakes, adjustments that come to terms with old conflicts and settle accounts, and alterations that enhance self-esteem and support a more optimistic view of life. However, revising the macronarrative involves more than just giving accurate voice to the client's life story. And clients must do more than amend their life portraits for accuracy. They need to modify the portrait to make it more livable. That is why they came to counseling. The process of coconstruction, with revision and elaboration, often begins with the practitioner saying something provocative. This statement aims to induce instability and opens the possibility for rearranging story elements. For a revised life portrait to move in the direction of stability, the process must be transparent to the client as well as invoke the client's self-conscious collaboration. Client and practitioner join together to candidly craft a move in meaning with which to confront choices. In so doing, the client repositions self in the emended life pattern. The new arrangement, of course, must be more viable and vital if it is to become useful.

The reward for looking back is the ability to move forward. The coconstruction of the life portrait seeks to incorporate the current dislocation in a way that increases the possibility of transformation and development. The limits of the client's language are the limits of the client's world. By reshaping their words, clients reshape their worlds. This includes accessing different meanings that restart stalled initiatives and absorbing new understandings that reveal fresh possibilities. It can mobilize the most central tendencies of the clients to chart a possible way forward. It often uses metaphors to open previously unnoticed avenues of movement. For example, having examined a life portrait of striving to be perfect, a client said she was ready to "take off my false face of perfection." Regardless of how novel perspectives emerge, they provide new language and expanded vistas with which clients may reorganize their meaning systems.

The reorganized meaning system usually clarifies priorities and produces new goals. Practitioners should ensure that there has been some elaboration and amplification of meaning by having clients articulate the new and enlarged perspective on their career story. Otherwise, clients may leave counseling with the same story and the same issues. So practitioners, at about the midpoint of the second session, listen closely to hear if a client's dialogue in some manner affirms an emerging sense of self, indicates a reorganized meaning system, and consolidates change in the identity narrative. This self-clarity will enable clients to make their intentions more apparent to themselves and the practitioner.

ARTICULATE INTENTIONS

About the middle of the counseling session, attention turns to articulating intentions. Intention precedes choice because it articulates the purpose that choice will pursue. Future intention brings together the past and present. The meaning embedded within intentions is central to the task of making choices and designing a life (Richardson et al., 2009). Clients bring a tension to counseling. The etymology of *tension* involves struggle. In this case, the struggle comes when a client's life story gets challenged and they must engage in identity work. Counseling turns *tension* to *attention,* or giving heed. As clients engage in autobiographical reasoning, they narrate what matters to them and how they might manifest it in work activities that matter to their families and communities. Counseling encourages them to view the dislocation or transition as an opportunity to revise the identity narrative or even start a new story line. Practitioners help clients to turn *attention* into self-regulatory *intention* by guiding discovery of their own values and life purpose. These images of self and personal development serve as guides and evaluative standards. Practitioners must help clients attend to what they already know and overcome the fear of becoming more of what they already are. When practitioners serve as witnesses for clients who speak about meaning and mattering in their lives, it encourages clients to articulate their intentions regarding possible selves and anticipations about future scenarios.

In the 20th century, vocational guidance concentrated on occupational choice and match making in the context of stable and predictable career trajectories. The 21st century psychological contract with employers offers temporary employment and uncertain career trajectories. Accordingly, career construction practitioners concentrate first on meaning making and intentional processes in the ongoing construction of self and lives (cf. Krieshok, Black, & McKay, 2009; Richardson et al., 2009), concentrating on the career theme to chart the next occupational plot episode. In knowledge societies, within which people will hold 10 or more positions during their careers, it is intention that guides the repetitive process of reflection and revision involved in choosing new positions. Intentionality serves biographical construction in times of uncertainty. During transitions, individuals should engage in autobiographical reasoning to cope with change and risk. Helping clients articulate their intentions clarifies the current choices to be made and enhances the ability to decide.

As previously stated, about the middle of the second session practitioners usually begin to concentrate on client intentionality by attempting to coconstruct a shared language of intention, or what H. Anderson (1997) called *coordinating intentionalities* through collaborative and generative dialogue. They try to bring forward intention from the life portrait by highlighting the central narrative—that is, the career theme and occupational plot. Working with clients to settle on the central narrative makes intentions explicit. It reveals the profound meaning and deep reverberation embedded in the plot issues the client brought to consultation. Settling on a central theme also advances construction of the identity narrative and provides clarity. As an example of the importance of this identity clarity, consider the 2008 presidential election campaign. Some pundits wrote that the eventual winner settled on a central narrative in his campaign, but his opponent did not. Mr. Obama identified himself as agent of change, whereas Mr. McCain wavered among self-presentations as a conservative, hero, maverick, commander, and straight talker. A clear identity narrative might have made it easier for the electorate to know who McCain was.

Practitioners help clients to settle on a central narrative for their occupational campaign by prompting them to write a sentence that summarizes their identity narrative. The idea is to crystallize into a compelling statement the narrative identity processing that they have just done. Practitioners might describe to clients that crafting this sentence involves writing their formula for success or their personal mission statement.

There are many ways to approach writing a success formula. Most career construction practitioners prefer to assemble phrases from the career story interview into a sentence that summarizes the central narrative in the form of future intention. They typically begin the identity sentence with "I will be happy and successful when I _____." It can be elaborated with process and outcome elements, or it may simply state the fundamental intention. In teaching beginning practitioners about success formulas, it is useful to have them concentrate on the client's version of a favorite story. Usually some phrase in the client's narration of the story may be used in drafting a tentative success formula. Practitioners typically compose two alternative success formulas before the second meeting with a client. These drafts come in handy if the client has writer's block. Around the late middle of the second session, practitioners present the sentence (or two alternative sentences) and ask clients to refine it until they feel comfortable with it as their success formula. Of course, practitioners do not have to prepare a success formula ahead of time. Instead, after revising the life portrait with the client, practitioners may ask clients to choose phrases and mold them into a mission statement. For example, one client selected from her identity narrative the phrases "solve problems," "help others," and "share feelings." She combined them into several alternative success formulas: "I feel successful and satisfied when I use my feelings to help others solve their problems"; "I feel successful and satisfied when I help people solve emotional problems"; "I feel happy and successful when I help people feel better about their problems." She eventually settled on the following identity statement: "I feel successful and satisfied when I help others solve their problems by examining their feelings." Practitioners who wish to rehearse a time-tested method for writing success formulas might try Haldane's (1975) model of dynamic success factors based on functional self-analysis.

DEVELOP AN IDENTITY STATEMENT

Distilling the life portrait to an essential statement of intentions in the form of a success formula or identity statement gives clients a better sense of pursuing their purpose. Some might say it expresses their "calling," especially if they realize that "the purpose of life is a life of purpose" (Leider, 1997). A sentence stating intention gives clients self-direction to refer to time and again when they face transitions or confusing choices. It also gives them something concrete to take home with them because they won't be leaving with an interest inventory profile sheet. With this statement of intentions in hand, it is time for the client to begin to author new choices that turn fluid feelings of indecision into solid possibilities to explore. Everything that is going to happen now is usually already present in the success formula. The future is embedded in it. The client's life portrait will sustain the process of decision making. The client and practitioner will now use the success formula, and if needed the complete life portrait, as a standpoint from which to view the concerns with which the client initiated the first session. Making intentions explicit in light of the career concern usually reveals opportunities and identifies possible actions that the client up until then had only glimpsed or implicitly felt.

9

Turn Intention Into Action

Near the end of the second session, clients should sense that counseling is concluding and feel an urge to act. According to Shakespeare (1891), "action is eloquence" (p. 64). And the necessary action is exploration of attractive alternatives. Having formulated a success formula, it is time to turn intentions into action. On the one hand, *intention* means having a purpose in mind as one acts. On the other hand, *action* means the infusion of behavior with meaning (Malrieu, 2003). Action inherently holds meaning from the past while it carries the person into the future. Through action, not decidedness, clients engage the world (Krieshok et al., 2009). Purposeful behavior seeks the information needed to firmly resolve the career concerns and settle lingering uncertainty. Action, not verbal expressions of decidedness, prompts further self-construction and life design. For some clients, the action needed to realize new scenarios is clearly evident and just requires them to do something they already understand completely. Other clients need to explore the possible selves and alternative futures that have been gathering focus and energy.

Exploratory activities are critical in the process of designing and building one's own life. By engaging in information-seeking activities, individuals come to learn which possible future they wish to pursue. These exploratory actions may even transform self-concepts and prompt reinterpretation of career themes. Action is required for clients to form significant conclusions about a scenario for the next chapter in their life stories as well as bring career counseling to a close. Systematic exploratory behavior, and reflection on it, enables clients to make choices that allow them to live what they know—that is, live their own story.

EXPLORE

To conclude the second session, client and practitioner typically devise an agenda for action that propels and directs the client's advance into the future. Together they plan actions that will help clients see choices clearly, thereby enhancing their ability to decide. Of course, the plan concentrates on actions that directly resolve the issues clients brought to counseling. The actions needed usually involve exploration. However, the required action may center on negotiating with family members about firmly held preferences that may disappoint significant others. I will discuss negotiating with an audience who is hesitant to validate a client's new story after considering the more common planning for exploration.

To encourage clients to explore, practitioners help clients plan actions that they perceive to relate to future expectations. Most clients do not know how to explore their choices and their probable consequences. Therefore, in conjunction with suggesting specific activities that will increase the clarity of their choices, practitioners must teach clients about exploratory behavior. They might do so by using a handout called "Examples of Information Sources" (Stewart, 1969). This three-page handout teaches clients how to explore and process information. The first page describes six basic information-seeking behaviors: writing, observing, reading, listening, visiting, and talking. The second page provides space to list how they will enact these six behaviors in exploring three alternative occupations, jobs, or academic majors. After executing these plans, clients complete a third page to record what they have learned and reflections on that information. Discussing the third page may be a good starting point for the next session.

Whereas the information-seeking behaviors of exploration are the same, clients seek different outcomes from exploration. The goals of exploration fall along a continuum from gathering general information to testing possible conclusions. Super's (1990) model of exploration names the sequence of tasks as crystallization, specification, and actualization.

Crystallize

For younger clients who are in earlier phases of their education and careers, the exploration plan usually details exploration in breadth. The tasks of broad exploration involve seeking information to crystallize preferences. Exploration in breadth seeks to turn an identity statement into a preference for a group of occupations, usually in the same interest field and at the same ability level. Crystallizing field and level preferences concentrates on the fit between self and occupation. Practitioners start to build a list of occupations (or academic majors) by naming clients' vocational interests, discussing the private meanings that these public interests hold, and explaining how these interests may be expressed in fitting occupations. In discussing how well various occupations serve clients' pursuit of purpose and implement their success formulas, practitioners should be as specific as possible and cite examples from clients' life experiences.

Occasionally, practitioners need help to generate a list of academic majors or occupations for clients to explore. In these instances, *The Occupations Finder* (Holland, 1990) or *The College Majors Finder* (Rosen, Holmberg, & Holland, 1987) usually proves helpful. More often than not, practitioners just identify occupational codes that accommodate the client's career themes and then circle fitting occupations grouped under those codes. If they actually discuss that list, then they give the booklet to the client to keep. One way or another, clients by this point have crystallized a list of fitting occupations to explore.

Specify

For clients with more life experience, the exploration plan may call for exploration in depth. These clients often have crystallized their preferences and narrowed their options before ever meeting a practitioner. Their search task involves more than fitting self to possible occupations in general. It involves the process of identity construction because in specifying a choice, individuals declare themselves before some audience. Stating an occupational choice constitutes a very public presentation of the self. It displays who one is and announces what one wants to become.

Advanced exploration of a few alternative preferences concentrates on specific pieces of information that clients need as reassurance before making a commitment. Sometimes the information is so specific that it requires a few simple actions. Other times acquiring the information takes more work, yet that effort is always highly focused. For example, a high school teacher with a master's degree in curriculum wanted to return to school to earn a doctorate. However, even with a crystallized preference for an education doctorate, she was unsure of which discipline to study. She was considering counseling or psychology. It quickly became apparent that she was interested in understanding how children learn. With little effort, she narrowed her alternatives to school psychology and educational psychology. She needed to learn more about each in order to compare them and then choose. So she read about each discipline on the Internet, visited faculty who taught in each discipline, and read academic journals in each field. When she returned to discuss her findings with the practitioner, she had already committed herself to doctoral study in educational psychology.

Actualize

For clients who have selected an occupation and now must decide on an organization or seek a position in it, the exploration plan calls for making the choice real by testing it. Actualizing a choice involves job seeking and trying on a position. These clients must turn their verbal choice of an occupation into an actual choice by securing a position in it. Trial connotes employment in internships, part-time positions that may become permanent, or entry-level positions. To actualize her specified choice, the client who had chosen to pursue a doctorate in education had requested application materials from five universities in three states. Then she explored in depth the four universities that admitted her, soon actualizing her choice by entering one.

DECIDING AND DOING

The next session, if needed, involves reviewing the outcomes of exploration and making tentative decisions. The actions taken and the information collected usually elaborate a client's thinking. The client needs to discuss the new distinctions and disappointments. Together client and practitioner examine various choices to clarify the client's opportunities and to estimate how possible futures might unfold. Some clients lean toward unrealistic choices that claim more than their scripts can sustain. To realistically examine alternative choices, the client and practitioner must attach consequences to each alternative. Once a client commits to a choice, it is helpful to elaborate this choice by outlining a list of actions that convert it into an actuality through weekly activities, intermediate projects, and long-term goals. These actions must occur in the real world.

Clients must perform their new meanings. However, for more than a few clients, the problem is not deciding, it is doing. They need to find courage to live the new story in the world. If a client can choose, yet hesitates to enact the choice, then practitioners attend to attitudes toward the choice and possible barriers that thwart action, which is typically normatively constrained. The attitudes, beliefs, and competencies needed to enact a choice are identified by career construction theory's model of adaptability. The dimensions of career adaptabilities are labeled *concern, control, curiosity,* and *confidence.* Deficits in any dimension lead to distinct difficulties in enacting a choice. Methods for assessing and remediating these deficits are discussed in Savickas (2005).

In considering barriers, practitioners attend to feelings, circumstances, and relationships that may block action. In this context, feelings may be considered constructs of transition (Kelly, 1955) because they express the experience of moving from an old story to a new story. The most common feeling that stalls movement is anxiety. Clients feel anxious when they know that things will change yet do not know what to anticipate or how well things will turn out. Some clients feel sadness because they have trouble letting go of the old story. Other clients feel angry because they cannot control elements of the transition. Still other clients feel helpless, so they want to depend on someone else to take responsibility for advancing the transition. If emotion blocks motion, practitioners may use client-centered techniques to explore feelings, determine the meaning, elaborate possible consequences, and detail first steps toward enacting a choice.

For other clients, it is not feelings but reality that thwarts easy action. Then, rather than client-centered techniques, practitioners may prefer to use solution-focused techniques. This social constructionist therapy concentrates on helping clients bring forth their preferred actions in difficult situations (de Shazer, 1988). A useful solution-focused technique consists of finding exceptions to the difficulty in "doing" and then examining when, where, with whom, and how pieces of that action are already happening. Practitioners attend to movements that break through the barrier, whether these moves are small increments or large changes. Together client and practitioner discuss what is different on occasions when action seems doable. By bringing these small successes to client awareness and encouraging clients to repeat the successful behaviors, practitioners help them move toward securing a preferred position. A second solution-focused technique is the miracle question (Metcalf, 2005). Practitioners ask clients to envision a future in which the problem has been solved and then to look backward from that future position to explain how they had solved the problem. The specific question asks clients, "If you woke up tomorrow and your problem was gone, what would be different?" Then practitioners prompt clients to consider what they would be doing by asking, "What is different, and what are you doing?" Client explanations of how they envisioned solving the problem most often provide a basis for goal setting.

If the barrier does not appear to be internal feelings or external obstacles, then practitioners consider relationship problems by examining how clients are performing their new story for their audiences. Practitioners always hope that significant others validate a client's career choice. Nevertheless, they must learn if the barrier to doing resides in family interactions. So they ask clients about how their audience receives the story. They want to determine whether the client's audiences support the choice and change. *Support* means validation, not approval. Clients need family support to be autonomous and self-governing. If the audience does not validate change, then the practitioner uses encouragement techniques (Dinkmeyer & Dreikurs, 1963) and assertiveness training to build client confidence and self-efficacy.

If feelings, situations, or relationships are not the barriers, then practitioners consider the possibility that the choice itself is the problem. Maybe the client has second thoughts or intuitive resistance to enacting it. If this is the case, then client and practitioner recycle to explore some alternatives that they had previously set aside.

Although the steps outlined herein form the framework for career construction counseling, veteran practitioners adjust the counseling dialogue to what a client needs at the time. The key point is that the counseling agenda always attends to what clients need and how they want it delivered (Neimeyer, 2004a). The ultimate goal is to encourage clients to choose and enter an occupation that is meaningful to them and matters to their community. They should be better prepared to play the lead role in their own life stories as they take actions to enjoy a more satisfying life.

CONCLUDING

At some point, a new scene in the occupational plot has begun, and clients sense a changed relation between self and world. As counseling concludes, practitioners summarize what has been accomplished together. They read aloud clients' response to "How can I be useful to you?" Then they ask clients whether that goal has been accomplished. This reminds clients of their authority over the consultation and its closure. Practitioners usually end with a few sentences that summarize what has occurred by consolidating the new story and describing how it relates to why the client sought counseling. Playing with the etymology of the words *tension, attention, intention,* and *extension* provides a succinct structure to explain to clients the outcome of counseling. They brought some tension to address in consultation with the practitioner. Together client and practitioner paid attention to that tension during the career story interview. Then they coconstructed a life portrait to make intentions explicit and extend intention into purposeful action that resolves the tension.

Practitioners themselves may reflect on what has occurred by applying Kolb's (1984) four-stage model of experiential learning. The consultation began by having the client narrate "concrete experiences." This was followed by "reflective observations" regarding the experiences. The reflections became "abstract conceptualizations" in the life portrait. Finally, "active experimentation" with choice and change occurred. Of course, the cycle begins again as the client actualizes intentions in the real world and gathers new concrete experience on which to reflect, conceptualize, and experiment.

PRACTICE CASE

A practice case serves to illustrate the career story interview, assessment routine, and counseling. Read the following interview data, and, if you wish, before reading further perform your own assessment of the client's self, setting, story, and strategy and then relate it to the initial reason the client sought counseling. Raymond was a 19-year-old college sophomore majoring in biology. In response to the question of how counseling might be useful to him, he replied, "I want to figure out why I am so depressed when I enter the science building." He reported that he had a 4.0 grade point average and that the biology faculty regarded him as their most talented student.

Career Story Interview

His first model was Abraham Lincoln because "he lost political campaigns yet never gave up," "got up and gave speeches," and "wrote speeches." Thomas Edison was his second model because he was "imaginative," was "practical," and "told other people what to do." His third hero was Walt Disney because "he came up with and built imaginative things." Raymond enjoyed reading *Time* magazine for its movie reviews and political section. He also regularly read *Jazziz* for articles about jazz music and musicians. His favorite television shows were the *Star Trek* series because they are "imaginative." His favorite story was the book *Winesburg, Ohio* (S. Anderson, 1919), which Raymond summarized as being "about a boy who works for a paper and wants to write." His favorite saying was "The unexamined life is not worth living." For an early recollection he reported,

> I remember that when I was little I had to go to the bathroom in the middle of the night. My mother came to my bedroom and took me to the bathroom. It was dark, and she could not see that she had set me on the toilet facing backwards. I tried to tell her but she would not listen.

We worked out three headlines for this recollection: "Boy Forced to Go Wrong Way," "Mother Won't Listen to Boy," and "Boy Faces Backward."

Assessment

In the practice case, we have the autobiography of a boy who wants to make himself heard. Practitioners might begin the assessment by examining the early recollection. Raymond had to go to the bathroom in the middle of the night. His mother placed him backward on the toilet seat and would not listen to him tell her that something was wrong. His headlines condense both his perennial preoccupation and present problem: Mother won't listen as she forces the boy to go the wrong way, and the boy looks backward. Of course, it turns out that the student did not want to major in biology, but his mother insisted that he do premed and then enter medical school. He is "in the middle of the night," depressed as he looks backwards toward his parental guide rather than forward to his role models. He is figuring out how to make himself heard, both by his mother and in an occupation.

Linking the early recollection to role models shows how he has built a self that will be heard by others. Considering the repeated words in his descriptions of his three models, it seems that he has designed himself as someone who might make himself heard by writing political speeches that are imaginative. Also, one may wonder if the reason that he does not switch majors may have something to do with not giving up. In describing Lincoln, his first and most important comment was that Lincoln never gave up. He may see himself as someone who faces adversity without quitting, in this case precipitating depression similar to his hero Lincoln. Soon we will learn how his script works this problem out.

Raymond prefers environments that are political and imaginative. He likes reading about politics and movie reviews and watching *Star Trek* episodes. It seems unnecessary to consult occupational information booklets. However, for sake of practice, the client's RIASEC (Holland, 1997) preferred work settings seem to be Enterprising and Artistic. Thus, the practitioner could select from *The Occupations Finder* (Holland, 1990) several jobs that combine enterprising and artistic activities such as journalist, columnist, commentator, author, critic, editor, copywriter, creative director, editorial writer, lawyer, politician, actor, technical writer, performing arts manager, advisor, and consultant. There appears to be a good fit between his self-concept and the work environments that he prefers. Note again that we do not find interest in scientific or investigative environments. So both his self-concept and environmental preferences are incongruent with his life in the science building as a biology major.

Raymond's desired script is to write for a newspaper, magazine, or a political campaign. He wants out of biology and into journalism or political science. It takes little acumen to understand how this script enacts the self-concept in a fitting environment. It is so clear that one wonders how Raymond did not see it for himself. Maybe it is because he looked backward to his mother as guide.

The advice that Raymond gives himself is to examine his own life. The practitioner now comprehends how the client does not readily acknowledge that he is a person who wants to write for a paper or political campaign. The client avoids thinking about it by looking backward. The reason for coming to counseling is quite clear—Raymond indeed wants to seriously examine his life and figure out his next move. Depression has kept him preoccupied so he does not have to examine the matter. The practitioner would eventually repeat to Raymond many times that now he must examine his life, which is indeed his best advice to himself. The examination will clarify the matter because his story is so comprehensible, coherent, continuous, credible, and complete.

The practitioner is now quite prepared to respond to Raymond's request for assistance in understanding why he becomes depressed when he enters the science building. The client is a misfit in the science building. His mother has placed him there, making him go in the wrong direction. He wants to change direction, yet the best he could do up until now has been to use depression to stop moving. The practitioner reconstructed this understanding in composing the following life portrait for Raymond's consideration:

> You want to figure out how to make yourself heard. To have others listen to what direction to go in, you want to develop your skill at writing and speaking. The reason you are depressed when you enter the science building is because it does not value or reward imaginative young men who like to write and speak. You may be honoring your mother's wishes as you go in the wrong direction toward medicine. It is hard for you to get her to listen to your dreams, which preserves things as they are. Instead of biology and premed, you may prefer to major in journalism, English, speech, prelaw, or political science. You might even be dreaming of becoming a speechwriter or newspaper columnist. You know that now is the time to examine your current life, but the outcome could require difficult actions. The "but" feels like depression, like you are in the middle of the night and have to go but cannot. Switching majors will be difficult, because you might feel like a quitter and you would disappoint your mother. No wonder you are depressed each time you enter the science building. You are buying time before you examine your life and change direction.

After reflecting on the life portrait, Raymond wrote the following identity statement for himself: "I am happy and successful when I convince others through writing speeches and articles." In examining his life during counseling, Raymond quickly acknowledged that he wanted to write, not do science. He could become a science writer, yet he was more interested in writing about politics or entertainment. So what stopped him from changing majors? Recall Kelly's (1955) idea of feelings as constructs of transition. Raymond feared his mother's disappointment and wrath. Raymond then explained that he and his father found it easier to go along with her than risk confrontation. It was her dream that he become a physician, and she was paying the tuition.

With three short sessions of assertiveness training and rehearsal, Raymond summoned the courage to tell his mother that he wanted to turn his life around. To his surprise, she accepted it well, as long as he turned to another prestigious field. The practitioner thought that the consultation had ended successfully. However, this was not the case, and the plot thickened. Even with his mother's support, Raymond could not enact the move. His trouble remained in the doing, not the deciding. His difficulty was that he still could not change majors because he viewed it as giving up, prompting feelings of guilt. Kelly's (1955) explanation of guilt feelings fit Raymond, who believed that changing majors would violate the core of his self-concept. Raymond hesitated to move in the direction of his life script because he would become a quitter.

During counseling, Raymond quickly came to understand that his private logic considered changing majors as an admission of weakness. However, this cognitive insight was insufficient to move him to act. It took several additional counseling sessions to encourage him to make the change. It was particularly helpful when he transformed the idea that changing majors would make him a quitter to not changing majors meant that he was giving up on his passion. In short, he would be quitting on himself if he did not change majors. This reorganized meaning freed him to move forward with confidence and enthusiasm. Years later, the practitioner learned that Raymond had graduated with a major in journalism, completed law school, and worked as a speechwriter for a prominent politician. His mother was quite proud. An additional illustration of career construction counseling appears in the case of Elaine (Savickas, 2005, pp. 60–68), and live demonstrations are available on DVD (Savickas, 2006, 2009).

CONCLUSION

Career counseling practitioners hope that clients leave career counseling having experienced a process of transformative learning that has brought them into contact with their deepest sense of vitality. If so, clients are able to narrate a more comprehensible, coherent, and continuous identity narrative. Buoyed by biographical agency and ripe with intention, they should be ready for action in the real world and prepared to deal with new questions that will emerge. So empowered, they begin to write a new chapter in their life stories, narratives that extend an occupational plot with a meaningful career theme. In the last moments of the consultation, practitioners say goodbye by encouraging clients to take a chance on the story that strikes them as most true about themselves. They usually repeat the client's favorite saying, believing that their own words will bring forth their lives.

Appendix:
Career Story Interview Form

A. How can I be useful to you as you construct your career?

1. Who did you admire when you were growing up? Tell me about him or her.

2. Do you read any magazines or watch any television shows regularly? Which ones? What do you like about these magazines or television shows?

3. What is your favorite book or movie? Tell me the story.

4. Tell me your favorite saying or motto.

5. What are your earliest recollections? I am interested in hearing three stories about things that you recall happening to you when you were 3 to 6 years old, or as early as you can remember.

Glossary of Key Terms

AUTOBIOGRAPHY Life history that assigns present meaning to past experiences (Weintraub, 1975). Compare to *memoir*.

BIOGRAPHICITY Self-referential process by which individuals organize and integrate new and sometimes puzzling experiences into their biographies.

CAREER COUNSELING Career intervention that uses psychological methods to foster self-exploration as a prelude to choosing and adjusting to an occupation. Because it requires a relationship between client and practitioner, it is typically provided to individuals. Compare to *career education* and *vocational guidance*.

CAREER EDUCATION Career intervention that uses educational methods to orient individuals and groups to imminent tasks of vocational development and ways to cope with them. The service may also be delivered in a self-directed format such as workbooks and computer-assisted guidance programs. Compare to *career counseling* and *vocational guidance*.

CHARACTER ARC Aspect of a theme that portrays where an individual started, is now, and wants to end up on some essential internal issue. It explains the impetus that moves the individual toward something missing in life, something that the individual needs.

CHRONICLE Sequence of events arranged by time that merely terminates, without narrative closure.

EMPLOTMENT   Arrangement of diverse incidents and different episodes into a whole that imposes meaning on the parts (cf. Ricoeur, 1984).

IDENTIFICATIONS   Form of internalization in which incorporated characteristics of role models are taken on and stored in the mind as concepts.

IDENTITY NARRATIVE   See *narrative identity.*

IDENTITY WORK   Interpretative activities of "forming, repairing, maintaining, strengthening and revising the constructions that are productive of a sense of coherence and distinctiveness" (Svenings-son & Alvesson, 2003, p. 1165).

INFLUENCES   Form of internalization in which introjected parental guides are taken in whole and stored in the mind as percepts. Compare to *identifications.*

INTEREST   Psychosocial tensional state between an individual's needs and social opportunities to attain goals that satisfy those needs.

LIFE PORTRAIT   Macronarrative that organizes a client's chief pre-occupations, self-conceptualizations, preferred settings, dominant script, and advice to self into a portrayal of the occupational plot, career theme, and character arc.

LIFE THEME   "Problem or set of problems which a person wishes to solve above everything else and the means the person finds to achieve a solution" (Csikszentmihalyi & Beattie, 1979, p. 48).

MACRONARRATIVE   Autobiographical identity narrative that inte-grates several short or minor stories into a grand story about the life, one "that consolidates our self-understanding, establishes our char-acteristic range of emotions and goals, and guides our performance on the stage of the social world" (Neimeyer, 2004b, pp. 53–54).

MEMOIR   Small story that reports particular events more or less objectively (Weintraub, 1975). Compare to *autobiography.*

MICRONARRATIVE   Short story about an important incident, signif-icant figure, self-defining moment, or life-changing experience.

NARRATIVE IDENTITY   "Internalized and evolving life story that a person begins to develop in late adolescence to provide life with meaning and purpose" (McAdams & Olson, 2010, p. 527).

PLOT   Explanations and ending that structure a sequence of events into a coherent whole with a beginning, middle, and end. The end or conclusion brings the narrative closure lacking in a chronicle or story.

STORY   Organization of events into a sequence.

THEME   Pattern woven by a recurring, central idea that provides the primary unit of meaning used to understand the facts of a plot.

VOCATIONAL GUIDANCE   Career intervention that uses inventories and information to match individuals with fitting positions. The service may be delivered to individuals or groups or even be self-directed such as in computer-assisted guidance or workbooks. Compare to *career counseling* and *career education*.

Recommended Resources

Clark, A. J. (2002). *Early recollections: Theory and practice in counseling and psychotherapy*. New York, NY: Brunner-Routledge.

Cochran, L. (1997). *Career counseling: A narrative approach*. Thousand Oaks, CA: Sage.

Csikszentmihalyi, M., & Beattie, O. V. (1979). Life themes: A theoretical and empirical investigation of their origin and effects. *Journal of Humanistic Psychology, 19,* 45–63.

Guichard, J. (2005). Life-long self-construction. *International Journal for Educational and Vocational Guidance, 5,* 111–124.

Kalleberg, A. L. (2009). Precarious work, insecure workers: Employment relations in transition. *American Sociological Review, 74,* 1–22.

Lawrence-Lightfoot, S., & Hoffman Davis, J. (1997). *The art and science of portraiture: A new approach to qualitative research*. San Francisco, CA: Jossey-Bass.

McAdams, D. P. (2008). American identity: The redemptive self. *General Psychologist, 43,* 20–27.

Neimeyer, R. A. (2009). *Constructivist psychotherapy*. London, England: Routledge.

Savickas, M. L. (2005). The theory and practice of career construction. In S. D. Brown & R. W. Lent (Eds.), *Career development and counseling: Putting theory and research to work* (pp. 42–70). Hoboken, NJ: Wiley.

Savickas, M. L., Nota, L., Rossier, J., Dauwalder, J. P., Duarte, M. E., Guichard, J., . . . van Vianen, A. E. M. (2009). Life designing: A paradigm for career construction in the 21st century. *Journal of Vocational Behavior, 75,* 239–250.

www.Vocopher.com: Multimedia library on career construction.

References

ACT. (2011). *World-of-work map*. Retrieved from http://www.act.org/wwm/index.html

Adams, A. (1936, March 15). *Letter to Stieglitz*. New Haven, CT: Yale Collection of American Literature, Beinecke Library.

Adler, A. (1931). *What life should mean to you*. New York, NY: Blue Ribbon Books.

Adler, A. (1956). *The individual psychology of Alfred Adler*. New York, NY: Basic Books.

Alheit, P. (1995). Biographical learning: Theoretical outline, challenges, and contradictions of a new approach in adult education. In P. Alheit, A. Bron-Wojciechowska, E. Brugger, & P. Dominicé (Eds.), *The biographical approach in European adult education* (pp. 57–74). Vienna, Austria: Verband Wiener Volksbildung.

Allport, G. W. (1961). *Pattern and growth in personality*. New York, NY: Holt, Rinehart & Winston.

Andersen, H. C. (2008). Aunty Toothache. In *The annotated Hans Christian Andersen* (M. Tatar & J. K. Allen, Trans., pp. 341–355). New York, NY: Norton. (Original work published 1872)

Anderson, H. (1997). *Conversation, language, and possibilities: A postmodern approach to therapy*. New York, NY: Basic Books.

Anderson, S. (1919). *Winesburg, Ohio*. New York, NY: Huebsch.

Arnold, M. B. (1962). *Story sequence analysis*. New York, NY: Columbia University Press.

Arthur, M. B. (1994). The boundaryless career [Special issue]. *Journal of Organizational Behavior, 15*(4).

Barzun, J. (1983). *A stroll with William James*. New York, NY: Harper & Row.

Beck, U. (2002). *Individualization: Institutionalized individualism and its social and political consequences.* London, England: Sage.

Berne, E. (1972). *What do you say after you say hello? The psychology of human destiny.* New York, NY: Grove Press.

Bohn, A., & Berntsen, D. (2008). Life story development in childhood: The development of life story abilities and the acquisition of cultural life scripts from late middle childhood to adolescence. *Developmental Psychology, 44,* 1135–1147. doi:10.1037/0012-1649.44.4.1135

Borders. (n.d.). *Shelf indulgence.* Retrieved from http://www.bordersmedia.com/shelfindulgence

Bourdieu, P. (1977). *Outline of a theory of practice.* Cambridge, England: Cambridge University Press.

Bradbury, R. (1987). *Fahrenheit 451.* New York, NY: Ballantine.

Brandtstädter, J. (2009). Goal pursuit and goal adjustment: Self-regulation and intentional self-development in changing developmental contexts. *Advances in Life Course Research, 14,* 52–62. doi:10.1016/j.alcr.2009.03.002

Bressler, C. E. (2006). *Literary criticism: An introduction to theory and practice* (4th ed.). Upper Saddle River, NJ: Prentice Hall.

Bromberg, P. M. (2006). *Awakening the dreamer: Clinical journeys.* Mahwah, NJ: Analytic Press.

Brooks, G. (2006). Brave new worlds. *The Guardian.* Retrieved from http://www.guardian.co.uk/books/2006/may/06/featuresreviews.guardianreview6

Bruner, J. (1990). *Acts of meaning.* Cambridge, MA: Harvard University Press.

Bureau of Labor Statistics. (2004, August 25). *Number of jobs held, labor market activity, and earnings among younger baby boomers: Recent results from a longitudinal study.* Washington, DC: U.S. Department of Labor.

Burke, K. (1938). Literature as equipment for living. *Direction, 1,* 10–13.

Canfield, J., & Hendricks, G. (2006). *You've got to read this book.* New York, NY: HarperCollins.

Carlson, R. (1981). Studies in script theory: I. Adult analogs of a childhood nuclear scene. *Journal of Personality and Social Psychology, 40,* 501–510. doi:10.1037/0022-3514.40.3.501

CBS. (2009, August 23). Don Hewitt. *60 Minutes Special.* Retrieved from http://onebigtorrent.org/torrents/5988/60-Minutes-Special-Don-Hewitt-August-23-2009

CBS. (2010, May 9). Bebe Neuwirth: At home on the boards. *Sunday Morning.* Retrieved from http://www.cbsnews.com/stories/2010/05/09/sunday/main6470211.shtml

Cervantes, M. (1976). Colloquy of dogs. In *Cervantes: Exemplary stories* (pp. 195–256). New York, NY: Penguin. (Original work published 1613)

Chartrand, J. (1996). A sociocognitive interactional model for career counseling. In M. Savickas & W. Walsh (Eds.), *Handbook of career counseling theory and practice* (pp. 121–134). Palo Alto, CA: Davies-Black.

Christensen, P. J. (n.d.). Quotes about story and storytelling. *Storyteller.net.* Retrieved from http://www.storyteller.net/articles/160

Christie, A. (1977). *Agatha Christie: An autobiography.* New York, NY: Ballantine Books.

Clark, A. J. (2002). *Early recollections: Theory and practice in counseling and psychotherapy.* New York, NY: Brunner-Routledge.

Clifford, S. (2009, October 12). Suing her label, not retiring: Carly Simon won't go gently. *The New York Times,* pp. C1, C8.

CNNPolitics. (2009). *Who is Sonia Sotomayor?* Retrieved from http://www.cnn.com/2009/POLITICS/05/26/sotomayor.bio/index.html

Cochran, L. (1997). *Career counseling: A narrative approach.* Thousand Oaks, CA: Sage.

Coles, R. (1989). *The call of stories: Teaching and the moral imagination.* Boston, MA: Houghton-Mifflin.

Condorcet, M. (1787). *Life of Turgot.* London, England: J. Johnson.

Crites, J. O. (1981). *Career counseling: Models, methods, and materials.* New York, NY: McGraw-Hill.

Crossley, M. L. (2000). *Introducing narrative psychology.* Philadelphia, PA: Open University Press.

Csikszentmihalyi, M., & Beattie, O. V. (1979). Life themes: A theoretical and empirical investigation of their origin and effects. *Journal of Humanistic Psychology, 19,* 45–63. doi:10.1177/002216787901900105

de Shazer, S. (1988). *Clues: Investigating solutions in brief therapy.* New York, NY: Norton.

Dickinson, E. (1960). *The complete poems of Emily Dickenson.* New York, NY: Little, Brown.

Dinesen, I. (1979). On mottoes of my life. In *Daguerreotypes and other essays* (pp. 1–15). Chicago, IL: University of Chicago Press.

Dinkmeyer, D., & Dreikurs, R. (1963). *Encouraging children to learn: The encouragement process.* Englewood Cliffs, NJ: Prentice Hall.

Disney, W. (Producer), & Luske, H. (Director). (1953). *Peter Pan* (Animated movie). United States: Walt Disney Studios.

Dreikurs, R. (1967). *Psychodynamics, psychotherapy, and counseling: Collected papers.* Chicago, IL: Alfred Adler Institute.

Eliot, T. S. (1963). *Four quartets.* London, England: Farber and Farber.

Erikson, E. H. (1968). *Identity: Youth and crisis.* New York, NY: Norton.

Famous Poets and Poems. (n.d.). *Edna St. Vincent Millay quotes.* Retrieved from http://www.famouspoetsandpoems.com/poets/edna_st__vincent_millay/quotes

Fivush, R. (2011). The development of autobiographical memory. *Annual Review of Psychology, 62,* 559–582.

Forster, E. M. (1927). *Aspects of the novel.* New York, NY: Harcourt Brace.

Frankl, V. E. (1963). *Man's search for meaning.* New York, NY: Washington Square Press.

Freud, S. (1915). Thoughts for the times on war and death. In *The complete psychological works of Sigmund Freud: The standard edition* (Vol. 14, pp. 273–300). New York, NY: Norton.

Freud, S. (1948). *Beyond the pleasure principle.* London, England: Hogarth.

Freud, S. (1953). New introductory lectures. In *The complete psychological works of Sigmund Freud: The standard edition* (Vol. 22). New York, NY: Norton.

Gadamer, H.-G. (1975). *Wahrheit und methode* [Truth and method] (G. Barden & J. Cumming, Trans.). London, England: Sheed & Ward. (Original work published 1960)

Giddens, A. (1991). *Modernity and self-identity: Self and society in the late modern age.* Palo Alto, CA: Stanford University Press.

Gorokhova, E. (2009). *A mountain of crumbs.* New York, NY: Simon & Schuster.

Gottfredson, G. D., & Holland, J. L. (1996). *Dictionary of Holland occupational codes* (3rd ed.). Odessa, FL: Psychological Assessment Resources.

Graves, R. (1993). *The Greek myths: Complete edition.* New York, NY: Penguin.

Guichard, J. (2005). Life-long self-construction. *International Journal for Educational and Vocational Guidance, 5,* 111–124. doi:10.1007/s10775-005-8789-y

Haldane, B. (1975). *How to make a habit of success.* Washington, DC: Acropolis Books.

Hall, D. T. (1996a). *The career is dead—Long live the career.* San Francisco, CA: Jossey-Bass.

Hall, D. T. (1996b). Protean careers of the 21st century. *Academy of Management Executive, 10,* 8–16.

Hancock, J. L. (Director/Writer). (2009) *The blind side* [Motion picture]. Los Angeles, CA: Alcon Entertainment.

Hanna, M. (1994, March 29). A little girl's role model in the comics. *Cleveland Plain Dealer,* p. 2-E.

Harris, J. C. (1881). *Nights with Uncle Remus.* New York, NY: Century Co.

Heinlein, R. A. (1961). *Stranger in a strange land.* New York, NY: Putnam.

Heinz, W. R. (2002). Transition discontinuities and the biographical shaping of early work careers. *Journal of Vocational Behavior, 60,* 220–240. doi:10.1006/jvbe.2001.1865

Hemingway, E. (1935). *Green hills of Africa.* New York, NY: Scribners.

Hodges, B. (2009). *The play that changed my life.* New York, NY: Applause Theater & Cinema Books.

Holland, J. L. (1990). *The occupations finder.* Odessa, FL: Psychological Assessment Resources.

Holland, J. L. (1997). *Making vocational choices: A theory of vocational personalities and work environments* (3rd ed.). Odessa, FL: Psychological Assessment Resources.

Hollis, J. (1993). *The middle passage: From misery to meaning in midlife.* Enfield, England: Inner City Books.

Holstein, J., & Gubrium, J. (1999). *The self we live by: Narrative identity in a postmodern world.* New York, NY: Oxford University Press.

Hunter, A. G. (2008). *Stories we need to know: Reading your life path in literature.* Forres, Scotland: Findhorn Press.

James, H. (1908). *The novels and tales of Henry James: The New York edition. Princess Casamassima* (Vol. 5). New York, NY: Scribner's.

James, W. (1890). *Principles of psychology* (Vols. 1 & 2). New York, NY: Henry Holt. doi:10.1037/10538-000

Jennings, C. (Producer), Selick, H. (Director), & Gaiman, N. (Author). (2009). *Coraline* [Motion picture]. Los Angeles, CA: Focus Features.

Jones, E. (1953). *The life and work of Sigmund Freud (Vol. 1).* New York, NY: Basic Books.

Joyce, N. (2008). Wonder Woman: A psychologist's creation. *APA Monitor on Psychology, 30,* 20.

Kahn, W. A. (2001). Holding environments at work. *The Journal of Applied Behavioral Science, 37,* 260–279. doi:10.1177/0021886301373001

Kalleberg, A. L. (2009). Precarious work, insecure workers: Employment relations in transition. *American Sociological Review, 74,* 1–22. doi:10.1177/000312240907400101

Kelly, G. A. (1955). *The psychology of personal constructs.* New York, NY: Norton.

Kermode, F. (1966). *The sense of an ending: Studies in the theory of fiction.* New York, NY: Oxford University Press.

Kinney, A. F. (2007). One witch, two dogs, and a game of ninepins: Cervantes' use of Renaissance dialectic in the *Coloquio de los perros. International Journal of the Classical Tradition, 2,* 487–498. doi:10.1007/BF02677886

Kolb, D. (1984). *Experiential learning: Experience as the source of learning and development.* Englewood Cliffs, NJ: Prentice Hall.

Krieshok, T. S., Black, M. D., & McKay, R. A. (2009). Career decision making: The limits of rationality and the abundance of non-conscious processes. *Journal of Vocational Behavior, 75,* 275–290. doi:10.1016/j.jvb.2009.04.006

Krumboltz, J. D. (1996). A learning theory of career counseling. In M. Savickas & W. Walsh (Eds.), *Handbook of career counseling theory and practice* (pp. 55–80). Palo Alto, CA: Davies-Black.

Krumboltz, J. D. (2009). Happenstance learning theory. *Journal of Career Assessment, 17,* 135–154. doi:10.1177/1069072708328861

Lawrence-Lightfoot, S., & Hoffman Davis, J. (1997). *The art and science of portraiture: A new approach to qualitative research.* San Francisco, CA: Jossey-Bass.

Lecky, P. (1945). *Self-consistency: A theory of personality.* New York, NY: Island Press.

Leider, R. J. (1997). *The power of purpose: Creating meaning in your life and work.* San Francisco, CA: Berrett-Koehler.

LeRoy, M. (Producer), & Fleming, V. (Director). (1939). *The Wizard of Oz* [Motion picture]. United States: Metro-Goldwyn-Mayer.

Little, B. R., & Joseph, M. F. (2007). Personal projects and free traits: Mutable selves and well-being. In B. R. Little, K. Salmela-Aro, & S. D. Phillips (Eds.), *Personal project pursuit: Goals, action, and human flourishing* (pp. 375–400). Mahwah, NJ: Erlbaum.

Loewald, H. W. (1960). On the therapeutic action of psychoanalysis. In *Papers on psychoanalysis* (pp. 221–256). New Haven, CT: Yale University Press.

Lofquist, L. H., & Dawis, R. V. (1991). *Essentials of person–environment correspondence counseling.* Minneapolis, MN: University of Minnesota Press.

Machado, A. (2003). *There is no road: Proverbs of Antonio Machado* (M. Berg & D. Maloney, Trans.). Buffalo, NY: White Pine Press.

MacIntyre, A. (1981). *After virtue: A study in moral theory.* Notre Dame, IN: University of Notre Dame Press.

Malrieu, P. (2003). *La question du sens dans les dires autobiographiques* [The issue of meaning in autobiographical narratives]. Toulouse, France: Erès.

Markus, H. (1977). Self-schemata and processing information about the self. *Journal of Personality and Social Psychology, 35,* 63–78. doi:10.1037/0022-3514.35.2.63

Masdonati, J., Massoudi, K., & Rossier, J. (2009). Effectiveness of career counseling and the impact of the working alliance. *Journal of Career Development, 36,* 183–203. doi:10.1177/0894845309340798

McAdams, D. P. (1993). *The stories we live by.* New York, NY: Guilford Press.

McAdams, D. P. (2001). The psychology of life stories. *Review of General Psychology, 5,* 100–122. doi:10.1037/1089-2680.5.2.100

McAdams, D. P. (2008). American identity: The redemptive self. *General Psychologist, 43,* 20–27.

McAdams, D. P., & Olson, B. D. (2010). Personality development: Continuity and change over the life course. *Annual Review of Psychology, 61,* 517–542. doi:10.1146/annurev.psych.093008.100507

McCarthy, M. (2007). *Strong man: The story of Charles Atlas.* New York, NY: Knopf.

McLean, K. C., & Breen, A. V. (2009). Processes and content of narrative identity development in adolescence: Gender and well-being. *Developmental Psychology, 45,* 702–710. doi:10.1037/a0015207

Meltzer, B. (2005). *Identity crisis.* New York, NY: DC Comics.

Meltzer, B. (2010). *Heroes for my son.* New York, NY: Harper.

Metcalf, L. (2005). *The miracle question: Answer it and change your life.* Carmarthen, Wales: Crown House.

Miceli, M., Mancini, A., & Menna, P. (2009). The art of comforting. *New Ideas in Psychology, 27,* 343–361. doi:10.1016/j.newideapsych.2009.01.001

Mill, J. S. (1990). *Autobiography.* New York, NY: Penguin Classics. (Original work published 1873)

Milton, J. (1940). *Paradise lost.* New York, NY: Heritage Press. (Original work published 1667)

Morley, J. (1918). *Recollections.* London, England: Macmillan.

Murray, H. A. (1938). *Explorations in personality.* New York, NY: Oxford University Press.

Myers, R. A. (1996). Convergence of theory and practice: Is there still a problem? In M. Savickas & W. Walsh (Eds.), *Handbook of career counseling theory and practice* (pp. 411–416). Palo Alto, CA: Davies-Black.

Neimeyer, R. A. (1995). An invitation to constructivist psychotherapies. In R. A. Neimeyer & M. J. Mahoney (Eds.), *Constructivism in psychotherapy* (pp. 1–8). Washington, DC: American Psychological Association. doi:10.1037/10170-018

Neimeyer, R. A. (2004a). *Constructivist therapy* (Series 1—Systems of Psychotherapy DVD). Washington, DC: American Psychological Association.

Neimeyer, R. A. (2004b). Fostering post-traumatic growth: A narrative contribution. *Journal of Psychological Inquiry, 15,* 53–59.

Neimeyer, R. A. (2009). *Constructivist psychotherapy.* London, England: Routledge.

Neimeyer, R. A., & Buchanan-Arvay, M. (2004). Performing the self: Therapeutic enactment and the narrative integration of traumatic loss. In H. Hermans & G. Dimaggio (Eds.), *The dialogical self in psychotherapy* (pp. 173–189). New York, NY: Brunner-Routledge. doi:10.4324/9780203314616_chapter_11

Neuman, Y., & Nave, O. (2009). Why the brain needs language in order to be self-conscious. *New Ideas in Psychology, 28,* 37–48. doi:10.1016/j.newideapsych.2009.05.001

Nietzsche, F. (1954). *Thus spoke Zarathustra* (W. Kaufmann, Trans.). New York, NY: Random House.

Nobleman, M. T. (2008). *Boys of steel: The creators of Superman.* New York, NY: Knopf.

Osipow, S. H. (1996). Does career theory guide practice or does practice guide theory? In M. Savickas & W. Walsh (Eds.), *Handbook of career counseling theory and practice* (pp. 403–410). Palo Alto, CA: Davies-Black.

O'Sullivan, M. (2006, August 11). Artist as curator: Another perspective. *The Washington Post,* p. 24.

Parsons, F. (1909). *Choosing a vocation.* Boston, MA: Houghton-Mifflin.

Parton, D. (2010, July 3). *Dolly Parton celebrates 25 years of Dollywood.* Studio City, CA: Hallmark Channel.

Pelley, S. (October 7, 2007). Bruce Springsteen. *60 Minutes.* New York, NY: CBS News.

Plato. (2007). *The republic.* New York, NY: Penguin Books. (Original work published 380 B.C.E.)

Polti, G. (1916). *The thirty-six dramatic situations.* Boston, MA: The Writer.

Powers, R. L., Griffith, J., & Maybell, S. J. (1994). Gender guiding lines theory and couples therapy. *Individual Psychology: The Journal of Adlerian Theory, Research, & Practice, 49,* 361–371.

Propp, V. (1968). *The morphology of the fairy tale* (L. Scott, Trans.). Austin, TX: University of Texas Press.

Proust, M. (1923). *La prisonnière* (La Bibliotheque de la Pleiade Tome 3). Paris, France: Éditions Gallimard.

Pryor, R., & Bright, J. (2011). *The chaos theory of careers.* New York, NY: Routledge.

Reich, W. (1933). *Character analysis.* New York, NY: Farrar, Straus and Giroux.

Richardson, M. S., Meade, P., Rosbruch, N., Vescio, C., Price, L., & Cordero, A. (2009). Intentional and identity processes: A social constructionist investigation using student journals. *Journal of Vocational Behavior, 74,* 63–74.

Ricoeur, P. (1984). *Time and narrative.* Chicago, IL: University of Chicago Press.

Riley, E. C. (1994). "Cipión" writes to "Berganza" in the Freudian Academia Española. *Cervantes: Bulletin of the Cervantes Society of America, 14,* 3–18.

Rogers, C. R. (1942). *Counseling and psychotherapy.* Boston, MA: Houghton-Mifflin.

Rosen, D., Holmberg, K., & Holland, J. L. (1987). *The college majors finder.* Odessa, FL: Psychological Assessment Resources.

Saratoga Institute. (2000). *Human capital benchmarking report.* Santa Clara, CA: Saratoga Institute.

Sartre, J. P. (1943). *Being and nothingness.* London, England: Methuen.

Savickas, M. L. (1996). A framework for linking career theory and practice. In M. Savickas & W. Walsh (Eds.), *Handbook of career counseling theory and practice* (pp. 191–208). Palo Alto, CA: Davies-Black.

Savickas, M. L. (2001). Toward a comprehensive theory of career development: Dispositions, concerns, and narratives. In F. T. L. Leong & A. Barak (Eds.),

Contemporary models in vocational psychology: A volume in honor of Samuel H. Osipow (pp. 295–320). Mahwah, NJ: Erlbaum.

Savickas, M. L. (2005). The theory and practice of career construction. In S. D. Brown & R. W. Lent (Eds.), *Career development and counseling: Putting theory and research to work* (pp. 42–70). Hoboken, NJ: Wiley.

Savickas, M. L. (2006). *Career counseling* (Specific Treatments for Specific Populations Video Series). Washington, DC: American Psychological Association.

Savickas, M. L. (2009). *Career counseling over time* (Psychotherapy in Six Sessions Video Series). Washington, DC: American Psychological Association.

Savickas, M. L. (2010). Re-viewing scientific models of career as social construction. *Revista Portuguesa de Pedagogia e Psychologia. Numero Conjunto Comemorativo, 33*–43.

Savickas, M. L. (2011). The self in vocational psychology: Object, subject, and project. In P. J. Hartung & L. M. Subich (Eds.), *Developing self in work and career: Concepts, cases, and contexts* (pp. 17–33). Washington, DC: American Psychological Association. doi:10.1037/12348-002

Savickas, M. L., & Lent, R. (Eds.). (1994). *Convergence in theories of career development: Implications for science and practice.* Palo Alto, CA: Consulting Psychologists Press.

Savickas, M. L., Nota, L., Rossier, J., Dauwalder, J. P., Duarte, M. E., Guichard, J., . . . van Vianen, A. E. M. (2009). Life designing: A paradigm for career construction in the 21st century. *Journal of Vocational Behavior, 75,* 239–250. doi:10.1016/j.jvb.2009.04.004

Savickas, M. L., & Walsh, W. B. (1996). *Handbook of career counseling theory and practice.* Palo Alto, CA: Davies-Black.

Schafer, R. (1983). Narration in the psychoanalytic dialogue. In *The analytic attitude* (pp. 212–239). New York, NY: Basic Books.

Schneider, B. (1987). The people make the place. *Personnel Psychology, 40,* 437–453. doi:10.1111/j.1744-6570.1987.tb00609.x

Schultz, W. T. (2002). The prototypical scene: A method for generating psychobiographical hypotheses. In D. R. McAdams, R. Josselson, & A. Lieblich (Eds.), *Up close and personal: Teaching and learning narrative research* (pp. 151–176). Washington, DC: American Psychological Association.

Schwarzenegger, A. (2001, May 3). *Steve Reeves, champion.* Retrieved from http://www.schwarzenegger.com/en/life/hiswords/life_hiswords_eng_legacy_366.asp?sec=life&subsec=hiswords

Scorsese, M. (2005, September 26). *No direction home: Bob Dylan—A Martin Scorsese movie* (PBS American Masters series episode). Retrieved from http://www.pbs.org/wnet/americanmasters/episodes/bob-dylan/about-the-film/574/

Shakespeare, W. (1891). *Shakespeare selected plays: Coriolanus* (W. A. Wright, Ed.). Oxford, England: Clarendon Press.

Shipman, C., & Rucci, S. (2009, July 9). Nancy Drew: The smart woman's role model. *ABC News Good Morning America.* Retrieved from http://abcnews.go.com/GMA/Story?id=8034954&page=1

Simon, S. (2005, April 2). *Danes mark Hans Christian Andersen bicentennial.* Retrieved from http://www.npr.org/templates/story/story.php?storyId=4571854

Singleton, J. (Producer/Writer/Director). (1995). *Higher learning* [Motion picture]. Culver City, CA: Columbia Pictures.

Spacey, K. (Producer/Director/Writer). (2004). *Beyond the sea* [Motion picture]. Santa Monica, CA: Lions Gate Films.

Stafford, W. (1999). *The way it is: New and selected poems.* Minneapolis, MN: Graywolf Press.

Stevens, W. (1952). The idea of order at Key West. In *The man with the blue guitar* (pp. 129–134). New York, NY: Random House.

Stewart, N. R. (1969). Exploring and processing information about educational and vocational opportunities in groups. In J. D. Krumboltz & C. E. Thorensen (Eds.), *Behavioral counseling: Cases and techniques* (pp. 213–234). New York, NY: Holt, Rinehart and Winston.

Subich, L. M. (Ed.). (1993). Symposium: How personal is career counseling? *Career Development Quarterly, 42,* 129–179.

Subich, L. M., & Simonson, K. (2001). Career counseling: The evolution of theory. In F. T. L. Leong & A. Barak (Eds.), *Contemporary models in vocational psychology* (pp. 257–278). Mahwah, NJ: Erlbaum.

Super, D. E. (1949). *Appraising vocational fitness by means of psychological tests.* New York, NY: Harper & Brothers.

Super, D. E. (1951). Vocational adjustment: Implementing a self-concept. *Occupations, 30,* 88–92.

Super, D. E. (1957). *The psychology of careers.* New York, NY: Harper & Row.

Super, D. E. (1990). A life-span, life-space approach to career development. In D. Brown & L. Brooks (Eds.), *Career choice and development* (2nd ed., pp. 197–261). San Francisco, CA: Jossey-Bass.

Super, D. E., Savickas, M. L., & Super, C. M. (1996). The life-span, life-space approach to careers. In D. Brown & L. Brooks (Eds.), *Career choice and development: Applying contemporary theories to practice* (3rd ed., pp. 121–178). San Francisco, CA: Jossey-Bass.

Super, D. E., Starishevsky, R., Matlin, N., & Jordaan, J. P. (1963). *Career development: Self-concept theory.* New York, NY: College Examination Board.

Sveningsson, S., & Alvesson, M. (2003). Managing managerial identities: Organizational fragmentation, discourse and identity struggle. *Human Relations, 56,* 1163–1193. doi:10.1177/00187267035610001

Taylor, C. (1992). *Sources of the self: The making of modern identity.* Cambridge, MA: Harvard University Press.

Thoreau, H. D. (1992). *Walden.* Boston, MA: Shambhala. (Original work published 1854)

Thurber, J. (1956). *"The shore and the sea": Further fables for our time.* New York, NY: Simon & Schuster.

Tiedeman, D. V., & Field, F. L. (1962). Guidance: The science of purposeful action applied through education. *Harvard Educational Review, 32,* 483–501.

Vedder, E. (2008, June 26). *VH1 storytellers: Pearl Jam.* Retrieved from http://www.youtube.com/watch?v=Z3hK-MqF6O4

Vygotsky, L. S. (1978). *Mind in society* (M. Cole, Trans.). Cambridge, MA: Harvard University Press.

Wallis, K. C., & Poulton, J. L. (2001). *The origins and construction of internal reality.* Philadelphia, PA: Open University Press.

Waters, J. (2006). Mr. Williams saved my life: Introduction. In T. Williams, *Memoirs* (pp. ix–xix). New York, NY: New Directions Press.

Weintraub, K. (1975). Autobiography and historical consciousness. *Critical Inquiry, 1,* 821–848. doi:10.1086/447818

Welch, J. F., Jr. (1992). Working out a tough year. *Executive Excellence, 9,* 14.

Welty, E. (1983). *One writer's beginnings.* Cambridge, MA: Harvard University Press.

White, H. (1981). The value of narrativity in the representation of reality. In W. J. T. Mitchell (Ed.), *On narrative* (pp. 5–27). Chicago, IL: University of Chicago Press.

Whitman, W. (2008). *Song of myself.* Miami, FL: BN. (Original work published 1855)

Williamson, E. G., & Bordin, E. S. (1941). The evaluation of vocational and educational counseling: A critique of the methodology of experiments. *Educational and Psychological Measurement, 1,* 5–23. doi:10.1177/001316444100100101

Wittgenstein, L. (1953). *Philosophical investigations* (G. E. M. Anscombe, Trans.). Oxford, England: Basil Blackwell.

Wloszczyna, S. (2009, February 5). Perfect heroine for hard times. *USA Today,* pp. D1–D2.

Worthington, I. (2001). *Demosthenes.* London, England: Routledge.

Young, W. P. (2007). *The shack.* Newbury Park, CA: Windblown Media.

Ziglar, Z. (1997). *Great quotes.* Franklin Lakes, NJ: Career Press.

Index

About the Author

Mark L. Savickas, PhD, is chair emeritus and professor in the Department of Behavioral and Community Health Sciences at the Northeastern Ohio Universities College of Medicine. He also serves as an adjunct professor of counselor education at Kent State University, where he has taught career counseling to more than 5,000 students since 1973. He serves as president of the Counseling Psychology Division of the International Association of Applied Psychology (2010–2014). For his work in career counseling, he has received the John L. Holland Award for Outstanding Achievement in Personality and Career Research from the Counseling Psychology Division of the American Psychological Association (1994), the Eminent Career Award from the National Career Development Association (1996), the Distinguished Achievement Award from the Society for Vocational Psychology (2006), and honorary doctorates from the University of Lisbon (Portugal) and the University of Pretoria (South Africa).

About the Series Editors

Jon Carlson, PsyD, EdD, ABPP, is distinguished professor of psychology and counseling at Governors State University in University Park, Illinois, and a psychologist at the Wellness Clinic in Lake Geneva, Wisconsin. Dr. Carlson has served as the editor of several periodicals, including the *Journal of Individual Psychology* and *The Family Journal.* He holds diplomas in both family psychology and Adlerian psychology. He has authored 150 journal articles and 40 books, including *Time for a Better Marriage, Adlerian Therapy, The Mummy at the Dining Room Table, Bad Therapy, The Client Who Changed Me,* and *Moved by the Spirit.* He has created more than 200 professional trade videos and DVDs with leading professional therapists and educators. In 2004 the American Counseling Association named him a "Living Legend." Recently he syndicated an advice cartoon, *On The Edge,* with cartoonist Joe Martin.

Matt Englar-Carlson, PhD, is an associate professor of counseling at California State University–Fullerton. He is a fellow of Division 51 of the American Psychological Association (APA). As a scholar, teacher, and clinician, Dr. Englar-Carlson has been an innovator and professionally passionate about training and teaching clinicians to work more effectively with their male clients. He has more than 30 publications and 50 national and international presentations, most of which are focused on men and masculinity and diversity issues in psychological training and practice.

Dr. Englar-Carlson coedited the books *In the Room With Men: A Casebook of Therapeutic Change* and *Counseling Troubled Boys: A Guidebook for Professionals* and was featured in the 2010 APA-produced DVD *Engaging Men in Psychotherapy*. In 2007, he was named Researcher of the Year by the Society for the Psychological Study of Men and Masculinity. He is also a member of the APA Working Group to Develop Guidelines for Psychological Practice With Boys and Men. As a clinician, he has worked with children, adults, and families in school, community, and university mental health settings.